Sunrise Inn
Missouri

A Collection of Signature Dishes
From Missouri's Finest

From the
Bed & Breakfast
Inns of Missouri

The
Guest
Cottage Inc.

Woodruff, Wisconsin

The Guest Cottage, Inc.
PO Box 848
Woodruff, WI 54568
1-800-333-8122
Please call or write for a free catalog of other books by the Guest Cottage.

ISBN#: 1-930596-11-1

Printed in the United States of America

Marketed by The Guest Cottage, Inc.
Cover art by Shelly Reeves Smith
Designed by Debra Adams

Contents

Participating Inns

Associate Inns

Map of Bed & Breakfast
Inns of Missouri

Guide of Participating Inns by City

Bed & Breakfast
Profiles and Recipes

Victorian Veranda

207 East School Street
Bonne Terre, MO 63628
(573)358-1134 or (800)343-1134
www.bbim.org/vicveranda
victoriaveranda@LDD.net

Hosts: Galen and Karen Forney

Victorian Veranda is an elegant Victorian mansion with a large wrap-around veranda. Choose from four romantic guest rooms, all with private baths. All four rooms have thermal massage baths for two, which you will enjoy after a day of hiking in one of the many parks close by. Relax in the parlor or cozy up to the fireplace in the gathering room. In the morning, the aroma of freshly ground coffee and a variety of home-baked goodies will guide you to the large dining room for a candlelight breakfast.

Rates at Victorian Veranda range from $85-$110.
Rates include a full candlelight breakfast.

Cheese Danish Crescents

This dish is a favorite with my guests and family. It came from my aunt. She owned a small restaurant where she served this to her family and customers.

makes 16-24 crescents

Dough:
2 1/2 cups flour
1 teaspoon baking powder
1 cup butter or margarine, cold
1/2 cup milk
1 egg, beaten
      OR
2-4 packages (8 ounces each) crescent dinner rolls

Filling:
1 package (8 ounces) cream cheese, softened
1 egg
1 Tablespoon lemon juice
1/2 cup sugar
1 Tablespoon flour

Glaze:
1 cup powdered sugar
lemon juice or milk

2 medium mixing bowls
2 cookie sheets
Baking Time: 16-18 minutes
Baking Temperature: 350 °

Dough:
In a medium mixing bowl, combine flour and baking powder; cut in cold butter until mixture is crumbly. Stir in milk and egg.

Divide dough into 3 portions; shape each portion into a ball. Roll ball out into a 12-inch circle; cut into 12 wedges.

Place filling in the center of each wedge and roll up from the wide edge. Repeat with remaining dough. Place wedges point side down on lightly greased cookie sheets; form into crescent shapes.

Bake at 350 ° for 16-18 minutes. Drizzle glaze over tops of hot crescents.

Filling:
In a medium bowl, combine softened cream cheese, egg, lemon juice, sugar and flour. Mix with electric mixer until smooth.

Glaze:
Combine powdered sugar and enough lemon juice to form a thin glaze.

Dauphine Hotel Bed & Breakfast Inn

100 Iris Avenue
P.O. Box 36
Bonnots Mill, MO 65016
(877)901-4144
www.dauphinehotel.com
info@dauphinehotel.com

Hosts: Sandra and Scott Holder

Discover Missouri's French heritage at the historic Dauphine Hotel, which has welcomed travelers along the Lewis & Clark Trail since 1875. Begin relaxing as soon as you arrive! In the summertime, take a stroll through our gardens and enjoy the numerous flowers and birds, or sit on the porch, listen to the fountain and view one of our spectacular sunsets over the Osage River. In wintertime, curl up in front of the stove in the lobby or parlor with a book from our library, or try your hand at one of our many puzzles and games.

At the end of the day, drift off to sleep in one of our seven guest rooms, all furnished with antiques original to the hotel. Awake to a hearty, country-style breakfast, then explore the shops and restaurants of Bonnots Mill, now a National Historic District.

Rates at the Dauphine Hotel range from $70-$100.
Rates include a full breakfast.

Beignets

These French or Creole doughnuts are famous in New Orleans, and they are wonderful with breakfast or as a snack. Early settlers in Bonnots Mill would have eaten these, having first arrived in New Orleans before traveling up the Mississippi and Missouri Rivers to Bonnots Mill. Serve hot with a cup of café au lait.

makes 2-3 dozen

1 package active dry yeast
3/4 cup water (105 °)
1/4 cup sugar
1/2 teaspoon salt
1 egg
1/2 cup evaporated milk
3 1/2 cups all-purpose flour
2 Tablespoons shortening
oil for fying

dust with powdered sugar, if desired

2 large mixing bowls
1 large saucepan or deep fryer
1 large serving platter or individual pastry plates
Frying Time: 2-3 minutes per side
Frying Temperature: 360 °

In large mixing bowl, dissolve yeast in warm water. Add sugar, salt, egg and evaporated milk. Blend with a beater. Add half of the flour and beat until smooth. Add shortening and beat in remaining flour. Place in a greased bowl, cover with plastic wrap and chill overnight.

Please note: This dough can be kept for up to a week in the refrigerator and actually improves with age—just punch it down when it rises.

When you are ready to fry the beignets, heat 3 inches of oil to 360 ° in a large saucepan or deep fryer. Roll dough out on floured board to a thickness of 1/8 inch. Cut dough into 2 inch strips on a diagonal. Cut again along the opposite diagonal to form diamonds.

Carefully slide beignets into hot oil a few at a time. Fry until puffy and golden brown, 2-3 minutes per side. Remove with a slotted spoon and drain on paper towels.

If desired, generously dust powdered sugar on the beignets while they are still hot. Serve with café au lait.

Rivercene
Bed & Breakfast

127 County Road 463
Boonville, MO 65233
(800)531-0862 or (660)848-2497
www.Rivercene.com
host@Rivercene.com

Host: Ron Lenz

Stay at the home of Riverboat Captain Kinney's mansion built in 1869. Retire to a spacious room with a queen size bed and private bath. For your complete renewal, discover a Jacuzzi for two. Recline on the porch or warm yourself by one of the nine marble fireplaces. Rest after your ride on the Katy Trail, antique shopping, walking or a trip to the casino. Start your day with a full breakfast and relax at this historic Victorian B&B in rural Missouri River country.

Rates at Rivercene range from $90-$150.
Rates include a full breakfast.

Mom's Blueberry Coffee Cake

A delightful start to a morning of relaxation and fun. This coffee cake is easy to make and easier to eat.

serves 12-15

2 cups flour
3/4 cup sugar
2 1/2 teaspoons baking powder
3/4 teaspoon salt
1/3 cup shortening
3/4 cup milk
1 egg
1 cup blueberries, fresh or thawed

Topping:
1/3 cup flour
1/2 cup sugar
1 teaspoon cinnamon
1/3 cup soft margarine

1 one quart mixing bowl
1 three quart mixing bowl
1 9x13 inch baking dish
Baking Time: 40 minutes
Baking Temperature: 350 °

Combine first 7 ingredients with mixer until smooth.

Stir in blueberries.

Place mixture in greased 9x13 inch baking dish.

Topping:
Combine all ingredients until crumbly.

Sprinkle topping over coffee cake and bake at 350 ° for approximately 40 minutes.

Aunt Sadie's Garden Glade
Bed & Breakfast

163 Fountain Street
Branson, MO 65616
(800)944-4250
www.auntsadies.com

Hosts: Dick and Linda Hovell

Aunt Sadie's has the perfect atmosphere for you to make those special memories, time and time again. Nestled in the midst of seven acres of timber, you will find that much needed peace and quiet, yet you're only minutes away from the variety of things that Branson has to offer. In your room/cabin, you will find a king or queen size bed, private bath, color TV/VCR, refrigerator, microwave, coffee maker, fireplace and your own private hot tub on a secluded deck or a two-person whirlpool in your room. After enjoying all of this, a full country breakfast is served family style each morning in the main house.

Rates at Aunt Sadie's range from $95-$150.
Rates include a full breakfast.

Branson Eggs Benedict

This recipe comes to Aunt Sadie's from a great friend and one of the best cooks that I know, Patti Scott. She has taken this recipe and added her special touch and ingredients to make it one of Branson's best.

serves 8

1 1/2 sticks butter
3/4 cup flour
4 cups milk
2 cups ham, cubed
1 1/2 cups Cheddar cheese, grated
12 eggs, hard boiled and cubed
1/2 to 3/4 cup cooking sherry
Cavender's seasoning, to taste
2 cups asparagus, cut into 1 inch pieces and blanched (optional)

Toppings:
shredded cheese
bacon bits
green onion

1 large saucepan

Melt butter in a large saucepan over moderate heat. Blend in flour, stirring constantly until mixture is smooth and bubbly. Gradually add milk. Heat to boiling, stirring constantly.

Turn heat to low. Add ham and cheese; stir until cheese is melted. Add eggs and asparagus. Stir in seasoning and sherry. Stir very gently while heating thoroughly.

Serve over sweet cornbread. Top with cheese, bacon, and onion.

Red Bud Cove
Bed & Breakfast Suites

162 Lakewood Drive
Branson/Hollister, MO 65672
(800)677-5525
www.redbudcove.com
redbudcove@aol.com

Hosts: Rick and Carol Carpenter

Red Bud Cove is perfect for honeymoons as well as small group events. It features luxury suites in a pristine lakefront setting—and we are only a few minutes from the many exciting attractions in Branson.

Our eight suites are large, beautiful and enhanced with many amenities. Each has either a king or queen size bed, kitchenette, television and large bathroom. Some also include a fireplace and two-person Jacuzzi, and most have either a lake view deck or patio. Guests also enjoy our fishing and boat dock, hot tub building, picnic area and beautifully landscaped grounds.

Rates at Red Bud Cove range from $87-$130.
Rates include a full breakfast.

Stuffed Ham Rolls with Cheese Sauce

Each year, I try out new recipes so I can add a few to my repertoire. About five years ago, I tried Stuffed Ham Rolls with Cheese Sauce. The recipe was great, but I wasn't sure just how good a recipe it was for breakfast. That is until I started getting requests for the ham rolls when my guests were making return visits. This is now our most requested recipe, and I now feel confident that it is a good breakfast dish. I serve it with a hash brown potato casserole.

serves 12 people (2 ham rolls each)

2 cups sour cream
2 cups corn bread stuffing
2 packages (10 ounces each) frozen, chopped spinach, thawed
24 slices thin deli sliced ham
cheese sauce (see recipe below)
shredded/grated Parmesan cheese
paprika

Cheese Sauce:
1/2 cup butter
1/2 cup flour
4 cups milk
1-2 cups grated Cheddar cheese

1 medium mixing bowl
1 medium saucepan (for cheese sauce)
1 large casserole dish (for baking ham rolls)
1 large serving dish
Baking Time: 30 minutes
Baking Temperature: 350 °

Cook spinach until thawed; drain. Combine sour cream, stuffing and spinach; mix well. Spread a heaping Tablespoon of spinach mixture on each ham slice.

Roll the ham slice and place seam side down in large casserole dish, leaving a little space between every two rolls. You can use individual au gratin dishes, if you wish. Cover the ham rolls with cheese sauce, being sure to cover all exposed ham to avoid crisping the ham during baking.

Sprinkle with Parmesan cheese and paprika. Cover with aluminum foil. Bake at 350 ° for 20 minutes covered, then an additional 10 minutes uncovered.

Cheese Sauce:
Melt butter in saucepan. Add flour; blend well until smooth. Add milk 2 cups at a time and stir until thick. Add cheese and immediately remove from heat. Stir until well blended and smooth.

Canna Cove
Bed & Breakfast

158 Cove Lane
Branson/Ridgedale, MO 65739
(877)877-3886
www.bbonline.com/mo/cannacove
canna_cove@lycos.com

Hosts: Chuck and Linda Allen

A quaint and quiet setting on Table Rock Lake, Canna Cove offers an atmosphere for relaxation and enjoying nature. The garden suite is a romantic room with a white, sheer draped bed, open flame stove and private hot tub on the patio. The nautical room has a full bath and access to a hot tub on the deck overlooking the lake.

Canna Cove Bed & Breakfast, established in October 2000, is the home of Chuck and Linda Allen. Located just 15 minutes from Branson, live entertainment and dining selections are bountiful.

Rates at Canna Cove range from $79-$119.
Rates include a full breakfast.

Canna Cove Pancakes

A wonderfully light pancake made special with the addition of yogurt.

makes 8 pancakes

1 cup all-purpose flour
1 1/2 Tablespoons sugar
1 teaspoon baking powder
1/2 teaspoon baking soda
1/2 teaspoon salt
2 eggs, slightly beaten
1/2 cup plain yogurt
1/2 cup water
2 Tablespoons butter or margarine, melted

1 medium mixing bowl
1 large mixing bowl
1 griddle

Combine flour, sugar, baking powder, baking soda and salt in large bowl.

Combine eggs, yogurt and water in medium bowl. Whisk in butter.

Pour liquid ingredients, all at once, into dry ingredients; stir until moistened.

Preheat griddle; grease lightly. Pour about 1/4 cup batter onto hot griddle for each pancake. Spread batter out to make 5 inch circles. Cook until tops of pancakes are bubbly and appear dry. Turn and cook until browned, about 2 minutes.

Castleview Bed & Breakfast

Rural Route Box 183 M
Camdenton, MO 65020
(877)346-9818
www.lakelinks.com/castleview

Hosts: Kathleen and Rod Allers

    With all its splendor, Castleview is still an informal retreat offering all the charm and hospitality of a first class Bed & Breakfast. We have created a restful "getaway" where you can escape the stress of our modern lifestyles. Relax in one of our four guest rooms with private bath or in our gazebo by the pond. Castleview has all the lake has to offer: boating, fishing, golfing, antiquing, shopping the outlet mall and many fine restaurants.

    But the real secret of Castleview is the jewel of the Missouri parks, Ha Ha Tonka State Park. Nestled next to the 3,000 acre park, you can enjoy Mother Nature in all her grandeur. Visit the old castle ruins, hike the many trails, explore the caves and enjoy the wildlife. From high bluffs to the natural spring to the beautiful savannahs, it will take your breath away. Then come back and let us pamper you with homemade treats like cream cheese brownies and lemonade or hot chocolate.

Rates at Castleview range from $94-$99.
Rates include a full breakfast.

Tofu Fruit Smoothie

Who would believe this is a heart healthy dish? It tastes like a thick, rich milkshake. Don't tell anyone that it is tofu until after they drink it. They won't believe it. We serve this as a fruit course to start the meal. When our guests learn how healthy it is, they don't feel so guilty about the decadence that follows.

serves 4

1 box (12 ounces) medium tofu
1/3-1/2 cup orange juice
1 box (16 ounces) frozen fruit, partially thawed (we like strawberries)
1 banana

1 blender

Blend tofu in blender until smooth. Add orange juice; blend. Add partially thawed fruit and banana and blend until smooth.

Bellevue Bed & Breakfast

312 Bellevue Street
Cape Girardeau, MO 63701
(573)335-3302 or (800)768-6822
www.bbonline.com/mo/bellevue
bellevuebb@compuserve.com

Host: Marsha Toll

The Bellevue Bed & Breakfast in historic downtown Cape Girardeau is on the local historic register and features four inviting rooms with private baths, two with whirlpool tubs. This 1891 Queen Anne Victorian features two parlors, a front porch and deck where guests can relax while sipping complimentary wine. The interior features original carved woodwork, stained glass windows and period ceiling stencils. Although the home has Victorian architecture and design, guests will find the interior light and comfortable. The morning room is named for its wonderful morning light where guests read the paper and drink coffee before breakfast in the formal dining room. Guests will particularly enjoy being greeted with Tollhouse cookies and fresh flowers and by the Bellevue Beagles, Arthur and Beatrice.

Just two hours from St. Louis, the Bellevue Bed & Breakfast is within walking distance of Cape's historic area, fine restaurants, the Mississippi River and Southeast Missouri State University.

Rates at the Bellevue range from $75-$115.
Rates include a full breakfast.

Lemon Butter Baked Salmon
with Mustard Dill Sauce

This is an elegant entrée that I first served at a small wedding brunch. The bride and groom make it for their guests now, and the recipe is one of my most frequently requested. It can be made ahead of time and served either hot or cold, depending on the time of year and day. It looks lovely on a silver platter garnished with green dill, lemon slices and cucumber slices.

serves 8-12

1 whole salmon (4-8 pounds), head and fins removed, scaled, cleaned
1 lemon, large
1/2 to 1 cup butter, softened
salt and white pepper
1-2 bunches fresh dill (optional)

Dill Sauce:
8 Tablespoons Dijon style mustard
2/3 cup mayonnaise
4 Tablespoons white vinegar
3-4 Tablespoons sugar
2 teaspoons dry mustard
6 Tablespoons dry dill weed

2 small mixing bowls
1 8 1/2x11 inch baking dish or large enough to just hold salmon
1 serving platter
Baking Time: 1-1 1/2 hours
Baking Temperature: 350 °

Make sure fish is perfectly clean and dry. Salt and pepper the inside cavity of the salmon and place a bunch of dill inside along with slices of lemon, if desired.

In a small bowl, blend the butter and grated lemon rind. With a broad knife or narrow spatula, spread the lemon butter over the outside of the salmon, going against the natural scale formation so the butter sticks to the fish on both sides.

Preheat oven to 350 °. Place fish in baking dish just large enough to hold the salmon comfortably. Make a foil tent over the fish so that the foil does not touch the fish but covers it completely. Bake for about one hour, depending on the size of the salmon. A 6 pound salmon should take about one hour; a smaller fish will take less, a larger fish more. The meat should be moist and tender, not dry.

When the salmon is done, remove the foil tent and transfer fish to a serving platter. Serve warm or allow to cool. Garnish with sliced lemon rings, sliced cucumber circles and dill sprigs. Pass Dill Sauce with salmon.

Dill Sauce:
Blend the mustards, sugar and vinegar in a food processor, blender or mixing bowl. Add the mayonnaise and dill. Taste. You may need to add more dill. The longer it sits, the tastier it gets. Store in a tightly covered container in the refrigerator. It will keep for 2-3 weeks.

Trisha's Bed & Breakfast, Tea Room & Gifts

203 Bellevue Street
Cape Girardeau/Jackson, MO 63755
(573)243-7427 or (800)651-0408
www.rosecity.net/trishabb
trisha@igateway.net

Hosts: Gus and Trisha Wischmann

Located only minutes from I-55 near Cape Girardeau, our lovely 1905 Victorian home is a haven of history and relaxation and a plethora of fine foods. Our guest rooms offer nostalgia, romance and comfort. Breakfast is an elegant gourmet experience complete with homemade breads, jams, home-picked fruits and luscious entrées. We offer packages that include an excursion dinner train with murder mysteries on board, in-room massage therapists, vintage car rides, golf packages and more! Corporate discounts, private parties and dinners are available. Come and browse our interesting gift shop.

Rates at Trisha's range from $55-$85.
Rates include a full gourmet breakfast.

Semo Crunch" Waffles with Cider Syrup

This quick and easy melt-in-your-mouth delicacy has a "secret ingredient". See if you can figure out what it is! (Hint: It is what sets these waffles apart as being light and crispy.) That's part of the reason why they are called "Semo Crunch". Call me to hear "the rest of the story" when you make your reservations!

makes three 8 inch square waffles or five 6 inch round waffles

2 cups Bisquick
1/4 cup oil
1/4 cup margarine or butter, melted
1 egg
1 1/2 cups club soda

1 medium mixing bowl
1 waffle iron
nonstick saucepan

Mix all ingredients together in medium bowl with wire whisk.

Pour approximately 1/2 cup batter onto hot greased waffle iron. Follow waffle iron instructions for heating and time requirements. Generally, use medium heat for 5-7 minutes for each waffle.

Cider Syrup:
3/4 cup sugar
3 Tablespoons baking mix
2 teaspoons ground cinnamon
2 cups apple cider, fresh or packets
2 Tablespoons lemon juice
1 pat of butter (optional)

Mix dry ingredients on warm in a nonstick saucepan. Stir in cider and lemon juice.

Raise heat to medium, stirring often. Let boil one minute.

Remove from heat. Stir in a pat of butter for richness, if desired.

Makes 3 cups. Store in refrigerator for up to 3 weeks. Great syrup for apple pie or cake, French toast or pecan pancakes. Makes a delectable ice cream topping.

Missouri Manor

1121 Ashland Road
Columbia, MO 65201
(573)449-4437
www.missourimanor.com

Hosts: Lyria and Ron Bartlett

With all the intimate charms of an English manor house, Missouri Manor serves also as a gracious center for entertaining in Columbia. The exquisite and sometimes whimsical surroundings invite guests to relax and enjoy the hospitality.

Built for prominent businessman W.T. Conley in 1930, this is one of the few surviving grand homes in the area. The cherry staircase, tile, fountains and perennial gardens serve as a gentle reminder of the warmth and charm of yesteryear.

Rates at Missouri Manor range from $100-$175.
Rates include a full breakfast.

Chocolate Heart Cookies

Missouri Manor hosts many weddings and receptions year round. These unusual heart shaped cookies get rave remarks. Everyone tries to guess what gives the chocolate its zip—the pepper!

makes 2-3 dozen cookies

3/4 pound (3 sticks) butter
1 3/4 cups sugar
2 eggs, lightly beaten
3 cups flour
1 1/2 cups cocoa
1/4 teaspoon salt
1/3 teaspoon ground black pepper
pinch of cayenne pepper
1 teaspoon ground cinnamon
almond bark

2 large mixing bowls
1 large baking sheet
1 pastry board
Baking Time: 8-10 minutes
Baking Temperature: 375 °

Cream butter and sugar until light and fluffy. Add eggs; beat well. Sift dry ingredients and add to mixture by hand.

Divide the dough into 3 rounds. Wrap in plastic wrap and chill for 1 hour.

Preheat oven to 375 °. Lightly butter baking sheet or spray with nonstick cooking spray.

On a well floured board, roll out dough to approximately 1/3 inch thickness and cut with heart-shaped cookie cutter. Bake for 8-10 minutes until crisp but not darkened.

Let cool. Melt almond bark in microwave and dip cookies diagonally.

These cookies are better if made ahead, frozen and thawed before eating.

University Avenue
Bed & Breakfast

1315 University Avenue
Columbia, MO 65201
(573)499-1920 or (800)499-1920
www.universityavenuebnb.com

Hosts: Willa Adelstein and Susan Schabilion

University Avenue Bed & Breakfast is truly one of Central Missouri's hidden treasures. Sitting along the eastern edge of the University of Missouri campus and in Columbia's historic and eclectic East Campus neighborhood, the "U" is a delightful and enchanting mix of Midwestern hospitality and turn-of-the-century style and sophistication.

Rates at University Avenue range from $80-$90.
Rates include a full breakfast.

Marcella's Soufflé

My aunt, who is in her 90s and lives in Washington, D.C., would always make this when we would come for a visit. It is easy to make and there were never any leftovers.

serves 4

1 pound cottage cheese (not creamed)
3 eggs, beaten
1/2 stick butter, melted
1/2 cup Bisquick
1/2 cup Cheddar cheese

1 small mixing bowl
1 one-quart casserole dish
Baking Time: 40-45 minutes
Baking Temperature: 400 °

Mix cottage cheese and eggs. Add butter and mix. Add Bisquick, then add Cheddar cheese.

Pour into one-quart casserole dish. Bake in a 400 ° oven for 40-45 minutes.

Good served with damson or hot pepper jelly.

Rock Eddy Bluff Farm

10245 Maries Road #511
Dixon, MO 65459
(573)759-6081 or (800)335-5921
www.rockeddy.com
hosts@rockeddy.com

Hosts: Kathy and Tom Corey

As guests near Rock Eddy Bluff Farm, country roads gradually narrow to a winding lane overhung with trees, opening at last at the edge of a broad valley. Here the scenery dominates. Here the river, valley, the wooded hills provide a magnificent perspective for each of the secluded guest cottages, cabins and the Tree House B&B suite. Each accommodation owns a unique flavor, featuring country antiques, queen beds and inviting porches for basking in the scenic surroundings. Here guests can select from several rural pleasures: canoeing from the private river access, fishing, hiking, nature watching…or simply tuning to the rhythm of the landscape from an Adirondack chair. If weather allows, guests may find themselves exploring country roads from the seat of a horse-drawn spring wagon with the hosts. Sunsets might be observed beside a wood fire, anticipating the comfort of sleep and the gentle sounds of owls and whippoorwills.

Rates at Rock Eddy Bluff Farm range from $75-$130.
Rates include a full breakfast.

Chicken Lasagna

This tasty dish stretches the definition of lasagna, perhaps. But with its own unique flavor, it never fails to please. Consider this recipe's different ingredients, such as asparagus and Hollandaise sauce. It has become a favorite of our family and of guests to our farm.

serves 6

2 packages (0.9 ounces each) Hollandaise sauce mix
1/2 cup butter
2 cups whole milk
2 cups finely chopped onion
3 cups sliced mushrooms
8 cooked lasagna noodles
1 pound skinless chicken breasts, cooked and cubed
1/2 teaspoon salt
1/8 teaspoon pepper
2 cans (10.5 ounces each) cut asparagus
3 cups shredded Cheddar cheese
1 cup Parmesan cheese, freshly grated
1/4 teaspoon basil
1/4 teaspoon oregano

1 skillet
1 9x13 inch baking dish
1 medium saucepan
1 platter
Baking Time: 35-40 minutes
Baking Temperature: 350 °

Cut chicken into cubes and brown in skillet. Sauté onions and mushrooms in butter until onions are translucent. Set both ingredients aside.

Prepare the Hollandaise sauce mix and lasagna noodles using butter and milk.

Preheat oven to 350 ° and grease baking dish with nonstick cooking spray.

Spread 1/2 cup of the Hollandaise sauce in the pan. Layer 4 lasagna noodles, chicken, salt and pepper, mushroom and onions. Add remaining sauce, asparagus, 2 cups Cheddar cheese and remaining noodles.

Top with remaining Cheddar cheese, basil and oregano. Bake uncovered for 35-40 minutes, topping with Parmesan cheese after 15 minutes have elapsed.

Savory Vegetable Soup

To give this recipe the plain old name of "vegetable soup" belies its truly unique and hearty flavor. Consider three slightly unusual ingredients: sweet potatoes, celery seed and cumin. Amounts of the latter two can be adjusted to suit your taste as you make this your own dish. While this recipe makes several servings, you'll likely find most folks eating two or three servings each.

makes 4 quarts—12-16 servings

1 large onion
1/4 cup butter or margarine
3 medium sweet potatoes, peeled and shredded
3 medium zucchini, chopped
1 bunch broccoli, chopped
2 quarts chicken broth
2 medium potatoes, peeled and shredded
2 teaspoons ground celery seed
2 teaspoons ground cumin
1 teaspoon pepper
2 cups light cream

1 large pot

In a large pot, sauté onions in butter until transparent. Add sweet potatoes, zucchini and broccoli. Continue to sauté for another 5 minutes.

Add the chicken broth and simmer for a few minutes. Add shredded potatoes and the seasonings; cook for another 10 minutes until vegetables are tender.

Stir in cream and heat through but do not allow to boil.

Another great recipe from Rock Eddy Bluff Farm:

Scones with Spiced Peaches

We often serve our own version of a full English breakfast to our guests. While that breakfast is served in nearly every British B&B, it is a unique treat to most Americans. These scones often accompany the English breakfast, and they are grand with tea at any time of day.

serves 8

3 cups flour
1/3 cup sugar
2 1/2 teaspoons baking powder
3/4 teaspoon salt
1/2 teaspoon baking soda
3/4 cup cold butter
1 cup buttermilk
1 teaspoon lemon zest

Spiced Peach Filling:
1 can (29 ounces) cling peaches
1/2 cup white or brown sugar
1/2 cup cider vinegar
6 whole cloves
3 whole allspice
1 cinnamon stick

1 pint heavy whipping cream, whipped

1 large mixing bowl
1 baking sheet
1 cutting or pastry board
1 medium saucepan
Baking Time: 20 minutes
Baking Temperature: 425 °

Combine flour, sugar, baking powder, salt and baking soda in mixing bowl. Cut up butter and add to dry ingredients. Mix with hands or pastry cutter (do not over work).

Add buttermilk and lemon zest until just combined and turn out on a lightly floured board; knead briefly. Form into a circle and cut 8 equal slices as you would a pie. Put pieces on baking sheet, brush with melted butter and sprinkle with sugar.

Bake for 20 minutes at 425 °, then cool slightly. Split each piece and butter one side. Add the spiced peach filling and whipped cream, cover with the butter side and top with more peaches and whipped cream.

Spiced Peach Filling:
Drain peaches. In a saucepan, combine sugar, vinegar and spices. Bring to a boil, then simmer for 5 minutes. Add peaches and simmer 5 minutes more.

Remove from heat, allow peaches to cool in the liquid, then drain.

Recess Inn

203 East Main
Ethel, MO 63539
(660)486-3328
www.bbonline.com/mo/recessinn
recessinn@cvalley.net

Host: Nancy Morford

The Recess Inn gives you an opportunity to step back in time and experience the three R's: resting, relaxing and reminiscing in an old historic schoolhouse. The setting in the quaint little town of Ethel, surrounded by the beautiful rolling hills of Northeast Missouri, only adds to the charm. Our guests are always pleasantly surprised. We love showing them what America has to offer away from the hustle and bustle of their busy lives. We strive to pamper and please and help our guests take away wonderful memories with them.

Rates at the Recess Inn range from $65-$75.
Rates include a full breakfast.

Sandy's Apple Dumplings

This recipe freezes well and is not only a great dessert recipe for luncheons or teas but can also be served for breakfast, especially during that time of year when fresh fruits are not as plentiful. This can go right from the freezer to the oven, so make them ahead and pull out only as many as you need.

serves 12

2 cups flour
3/4 cup solid shortening
2 Tablespoons cream or half-and-half
1/4 cup boiling water
4 Granny Smith or Jonathan apples, quartered or cut in thirds,
        depending on size
1 cup white sugar
1/2 Tablespoon cinnamon

Topping:
1 cup white sugar
3/4 cup water
1/2 stick butter
1/2 teaspoon cinnamon (optional)
2-3 red hots (optional)

1 medium mixing bowl
pastry cutter
1 9x13 inch glass pan
Baking Time: 45-60 minutes
Baking Temperature: 375 °

Place flour in bowl. Using a pastry cutter, cut in shortening. With a fork, stir in cream then water. Roll pastry out between 2 sheets of wax paper.

Peel, core and quarter apples. Combine the sugar and cinnamon, and roll the apples in this mixture before diapering it with strips of the warm pastry.

Place in freezer bags and freeze until ready to use.

Topping:
Combine all ingredients and cook on stove until sugar dissolves and starts to boil.

Pour over frozen diapered apples that are set in glass pan. Bake uncovered for 45-60 minutes in a 375 ° oven.

The Red Oak Inn
Bed & Breakfast

1046 Red Oak Road
Fordland, MO 65652
(417)767-2444
www.TheRedOakInn.com
frontdesk@TheRedOakInn.com

Hosts: Carol and Larry Alberty

The Red Oak Inn is truly a romantic country bed & breakfast. This charming three-story structure is a renovated dairy barn meticulously transformed into a blissful refuge with timeless appeal. It hosts five guest rooms distinctly decorated with different themes. Each room has its own private bath. There are three different setting rooms, a sun room where breakfast is served (weather permitting), the kitchen area with a wood burning fireplace where you may have breakfast in the winter. For your relaxation, there is an outside hot tub, a gazebo and the wrap around porches with rockers to entice visitors into practicing the gentle art of porching. There are also hammocks and swings for your enjoyment. Whatever you decide, there is a spot for you to enjoy and forget your cares in a friendly and relaxed atmosphere.

Rates at The Red Oak Inn range from $80-$85.
Rates include a full breakfast.

Chicken-Pecan Quiche

This recipe is great for a lady's luncheon, served with a spring mixture salad, fruit and muffins.

serves 6-8

---

1 cup all-purpose flour
1 cup shredded Cheddar cheese
3/4 cup chopped pecans
1/2 teaspoon salt
1/4 teaspoon paprika
1/3 cup vegetable oil
3 eggs, beaten
1 carton (8 ounces) sour cream
1/4 cup mayonnaise
1/2 cup chicken broth
2 cups cooked chicken, chopped
1 Tablespoon minced onion
1/2 cup shredded sharp Cheddar cheese
1/2 teaspoon dried dill weed
3 drops hot sauce
1/2 cup pecan halves

1 large mixing bowl
1 9-inch quiche dish
Baking Time: 45 minutes
Baking Temperature: 325 °

Combine flour and next four ingredients in a bowl; stir in oil. Set aside 1/4 of the mixture. Press remaining mixture in bottom and up the sides of a 9-inch quiche pan. Prick bottom and sides with fork. Bake for 10 minutes at 350 °.

Combine eggs, sour cream, mayonnaise and chicken broth. Stir in chicken, sharp Cheddar cheese, onion, dill weed, and hot sauce. Pour into prepared crust. Sprinkle reserved crumb mixture over filling; top with pecan halves.

Bake at 325 ° for 45 minutes. Serve immediately.

Loganberry Inn

310 West Seventh Street
Fulton, MO 65251
(573)642-9229
www.loganberryinn.com
loganberry@socket.net

Hosts: Cathy and Carl McGeorge

The Loganberry Inn is a grand Victorian built in 1899 in historic Fulton. The inn has had many famous guests from all over the world, including Margaret Thatcher and her Scotland Yard detectives and Polish President Lech Walesa. The Loganberry, with its stained glass and marble fireplaces, is graciously decorated and furnished with English and French antiques. The inn has many amenities including down comforters, gourmet breakfasts (in bed, if you wish), fine linens, robes and slippers, ultra spa tub and fireplaces. Cathy's special recipe Chocolate Chip Cookies are served on arrival. The inn is within strolling distance to great restaurants, tea room, shops and downtown attractions. The Loganberry Inn also hosts murder mysteries.

Rates at Loganberry Inn range from $75-$160.
Rates include a full breakfast.

Lemon Ricotta Pancakes

This recipe makes very tender, very fragrant pancakes. I stack the pancakes, surround them with fresh blackberries, dust them with powdered sugar, accent with lemon zest and pour on real maple syrup. Very yummy!

serves 4

1 1/3 cups Ricotta cheese
3 eggs, beaten lightly
3 Tablespoons sugar
2 Tablespoons butter, melted
2 teaspoons lemon juice
1 Tablespoon lemon zest
1/2 cup milk
1 cup flour
1 teaspoon baking powder
dash of salt

1 medium mixing bowl

In bowl, mix cheese, eggs, sugar, butter, lemon juice, and lemon zest until smooth.

Add flour, baking powder and salt just until blended.

Cook pancakes on preheated 325 ° griddle.

Garth Woodside Mansion
Bed & Breakfast and Cottage

11069 New London Road
Hannibal, MO 63401
(573)221-2789
www.garthmansion.com
GreatBreakfasts@garthmansion.com

Hosts: Colonel (ret.) John and Julie Rolsen

In May 1882, Samuel Clemens (Mark Twain) traveled the Mississippi River, refreshing his memory while writing *Life on the Mississippi*. When he reached Hannibal, he quickly became a guest of the Garths at their Woodside Mansion. He wrote to his wife, Olivia, "I spent my nights with John and Helen Garth three miles from town, in their spacious and beautiful house."

Come and stay where Mark Twain chose as *his* Bed & Breakfast. You can choose to stay in the mansion with all of its grandeur or stay in the cottage for the ultimate in privacy.

Rates at Garth Woodside Mansion range from $109-$295.
Rates include a full breakfast.

Scottish Eggs with Mango Chutney Cream Sauce

These eggs are so nice to make and can be made the day before serving and kept in the refrigerator until ready to bake. They may take an extra 5 minutes if they are made the day before. They can be served hot, cold or at room temperature. We serve them hot at the mansion.

serves 8

6 eggs, whole
2 eggs, beaten
2 pounds fresh sausage
1/2 cup onion, grated
1/2 carrot, grated
3 cups toasted bread crumbs

Sauce:
1 cup sour cream
1/2 cup plain yogurt
3 Tablespoons mango chutney
2 teaspoons cumin
1 teaspoon curry powder

To prepare sauce, mix all ingredients together and serve on the side.

1 - 4 to 5 quart mixing bowl
1 - 4 quart saucepan
1 ice cream scoop
1 10x15 inch baking sheet covered with foil for easier cleaning
Baking Time: 30-40 minutes
Baking Temperature: 350 °

Place six eggs in cold water in saucepan. Bring to a boil; cover and turn off heat. Let set on the burner for 15 minutes. Cool eggs in cold water and peel. Set aside.

In the mixing bowl, mix the sausage, onion and carrot by hand until well combined. Using an ice cream scoop, separate sausage into 8-1/4 pound sausage sections. Mold each section around the egg, keeping the shape of the egg.

Roll these in the beaten egg mixture. Roll and cover with bread crumbs. This recipe can be refrigerated at this time.

Place on baking sheet and bake in center of preheated oven. Remove from oven and let cool slightly. You can then slice into 5-6 slices and fan out on the plate for presentation.

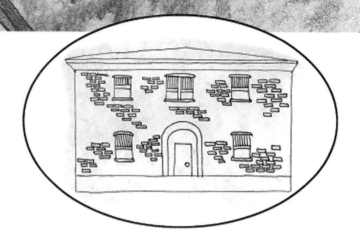

LulaBelle's

111 Bird
Hannibal, MO 63401
(573)221-6662
www.lulabelles.com
24dinr@nemonet.com

Hosts: Mike and Pam Ginsberg

"111 Bird" is an address with a long and infamous history. Built in 1917 by an enterprising madam from Chicago, LulaBelle's was the only Missouri bordello designed for its intended purpose. Today we offer fine dining in our first floor restaurant. Upstairs, rooms include heart shaped Jacuzzi tubs and Mississippi River views.

Rates at LulaBelle's range from $60-$175.
Rates include a full breakfast.

Corn Bread Breakfast Bake

A complete one-pan breakfast. A good way to use up leftover baked potatoes. Serve with f

serves 6

1 pound sausage
6 large eggs, beaten
1 can (15 ounces) cream corn
2 eggs, beaten
1 cup yellow corn meal
1/2 teaspoon baking soda
1 teaspoon salt
1/2 cup vegetable oil
1 cup milk
8 ounces Cheddar cheese, grated
1 large onion, chopped
3 baked potatoes, diced

1 medium mixing bowl
1 medium cast iron skillet
Baking Time: 45 minutes
Baking Temperature: 350 °

Preheat oven to 350 °. Brown sausage and onion in skillet; drain and set aside. Scramble 6 eggs in same skillet; set aside.

Combine next 7 ingredients in bowl; mix well.

Grease the cast iron skillet. Pour half of the corn mixture into skillet. Layer cheese, sausage, onion, scrambled eggs and potatoes in skillet. Top with remaining corn mixture.

Bake for 45 minutes or until lightly brown and pulling away from sides.

This is good with salsa or pico de gallo on top.

Reagan's Queen Anne Bed & Breakfast

313 North Fifth Street
Hannibal, MO 63401
(573)221-0774
www.bbhost.com/reagansqueenanne/
rqueenanne@sbcglobal.net

Hosts: Judy and Norm Reagan

Norm and Judy Reagan, owners of Reagan's Queen Anne B&B, invite you to come and enjoy their Victorian Queen. Filled with many 19th century antiques and family heirlooms, guests are certain to feel as if they have entered into a fascinating bygone era. The original oak gingerbread partitions greet guests as they step into the foyer, complete with black and white checkerboard floor tiles. Upon entering, your eyes are immediately drawn to one of the exquisitely carved, original fireplace mantles in dual parlors to either side of the entrance. The home retains the original Rookwood ceramic tiles, which surround the fireplaces, along with the original gas/electric chandeliers and beautiful stained glass windows. This old girl has been carefully restored and maintained and is listed on the National Register of Historic Places. The home is located in the Central Park Historic District of Hannibal, boyhood home of Samuel Clemens. The Reagans, along with Sam, or Mark Twain as he is affectionately known, invite you to come to the Mississippi River valley and experience the sleepy little town which inspired the writings of this famous author.

An 1880's Painted Lady and Victorian Jewel, Reagan's Queen Anne Bed & Breakfast is a glowing example of 19th century beauty and grace. Built by Wilson B. Pettibone, Hannibal's greatest philanthropist and lumber baron of the time, this three story home stands proudly on north Fifth Street as a reminder of Hannibal's prosperous past. Certainly Mark Twain, having spent much of his boyhood just two short blocks away, must have frequented many of the Victorian homes on north Fifth and the area of Hannibal which was known as "Millionaire's Row".

Rates at Reagan's Queen Anne range from $90-$145.
Rates include a full breakfast.

44

Fifth Street Peaches & Crème Muffins

Fifth Street Peaches & Crème Muffins is a recipe which has been a carefully guarded secret long enough. Many of our guests will be surprised and certainly delighted to finally see our signature muffin recipe in print. We are happy to share it with you, and we hope that you will visit Reagan's Queen Anne soon and try some of our other delectable fare.

makes 6 large muffins

2 cups all-purpose flour
3/4 cup sugar
3 teaspoons baking powder
1/2 teaspoon salt
2 large eggs, slightly beaten
1/2 cup unsalted butter, melted-do not use margarine
1 teaspoon vanilla extract
1 cup chopped peaches, frozen preferred
nonstick cooking spray

Crème filling:
1/3 cup sour crème
2 teaspoons sugar
1 teaspoon vanilla extract

3 small mixing bowls
2 medium mixing bowls
1 large (6 cup) muffin tin
Baking Time: 30 minutes
Baking Temperature: 350 °

Preparation of crème filling: Mix sour crème, sugar and vanilla until smooth. Refrigerate.

Combine dry ingredients in medium mixing bowl and set aside. Melt butter in small bowl in microwave and set aside to cool until just warm or it will cook the eggs when added.

In a small bowl, beat eggs slightly and add vanilla; set aside. After butter has cooled, add egg mixture and combine. Set aside. Chop frozen peaches into 1/2 inch cubes and return to freezer.

Preheat oven to 350 °. Prepare crème filling as listed above. Mix dry ingredients with butter/egg mixture and combine only until moistened. Do not over mix. Fold in frozen peaches.

Spray large muffin tins with nonstick cooking spray and fill each cup 1/3 full. Make a small indentation in the center of the batter in each cup and spoon 1 teaspoon of crème filling into each indentation. Top each cup with remaining batter until 2/3 full.

Bake for 25-30 minutes or until top is golden brown. An inserted toothpick will NOT come out clean, so test by touching top with finger to see if it springs back a bit. Let stand for 5 minutes before removing from tin.

Best served hot; there is no need to serve with butter.

Nestle Inn River Suites
& Guest Houses

215 West Second Street
Hermann, MO 65041
(573)486-1111 or (314)973-7090
www.nestleinn.com
Nestle@KTIS.net

Host: Donna Nestle

Nestled cozily atop a bluff overlooking the scenic Missouri River, two charming homes are the perfect getaway for romance and relaxation. Walk to Hermann's famous wineries, explore antique shops and museums and discover a unique world of comfort and charm created by innkeeper Donna Nestle just for you.

All rooms have refrigerators, microwaves and color television with cable. The romantic first-floor room and one of the suites have fireplaces, jetted tubs and king size beds. Spacious second-floor suites have fireplaces and king or queen size beds. Guests are invited to enjoy the hot tub.

The inn offers a spectacular view of the Missouri River. Delicious, homemade breakfast is available daily. Guest bike pick-up is available, and children are always welcome.

Rates at the Nestle Inn are $135.
Rates include a full breakfast.

Nestle Inn Egg Dish

This simple egg dish will have your family and guests begging for more. It is easy to modify the dish to the tastes of your guests.

serves 4-6

3 eggs
3/4 cup flour
1 cup milk
sprinkle of pepper
dash of seasoning salt

Choose from the following ingredients or add your own:
1/2 cup chopped tomatoes
1/2 cup chopped onions
1/2 cup chopped peppers (best with red or yellow)
1/2 cup grated squash or chopped spinach
1/2 cup chopped meat
1/3 cup grated cheese

1 medium mixing bowl
1 pie pan
Baking Time: 25-30 minutes
Baking Temperature: 400 °

Mix the first 5 ingredients in a bowl. Add your choice(s) of the vegetables and meat as desired.

Pour into greased pie pan. Bake at 400 ° for 25-30 minutes or until done.

Remove from oven and top with cheese. Return pan to oven only until cheese is melted.

Serve immediately.

Cameron's Crag
Bed & Breakfast

738 Acacia Club Road   PO Box 526
Hollister, MO 65672   Point Lookout, MO 65726
(417)335-8134 or (800)933-8529
www.camerons-crag.com
mgcameron@aol.com

Hosts: Kay and Glen Cameron

Cameron's Crag is a special Bed & Breakfast in a contemporary home and detached guest house. Perched high on a bluff overlooking Lake Taneycomo and Branson's skyline, all four of the guest areas offer spectacular scenery, a private entrance, a king size bed, private bath with a tub and shower, and a private and secluded hot tub. We are just three miles from Branson.

Rates at Cameron's Crag range from $85-$135.
Rates include a full breakfast.

Unfolded Omelet

serves 6

nonstick cooking spray
1 Tablespoon butter
12 eggs
1/4 cup sour cream
1/2 cup cottage cheese
2 dashes of Mrs. Dash

Toppings:
any combination of the following:
1 cup cooked sausage
1 cup chopped ham
Canadian bacon

1/2 cup grated cheese (Swiss, Cheddar, Monterey Jack, or a combination)

Optional Toppings:
cooked mushrooms
sliced tomatoes
red and green peppers (especially nice for Christmas)

1 medium mixing bowl
1 12 inch heavy skillet with lid
1 14 inch plate
Cooking Time: 30 minutes

Spray a 12 inch heavy skillet with nonstick cooking spray and melt butter on low heat. Combine the other ingredients in a medium mixing bowl. Pour egg mixture into skillet and reduce heat to low. Cover with a lid; a glass lid is best so you can see when mixture is set. This skillet is larger than the burner, so you'll probably need to move the skillet to finish cooking. Cook slowly for about 30 minutes or until egg mixture is set.

When omelet is set, top with choice of meat toppings in an attractive pattern. Top with grated cheese. Return to heat until cheese is melted.

Carefully loosen omelet from the pan. Choose a large serving plate, one that is 2 inches larger than the skillet. Hold the skillet above the serving plate. Starting about 1 inch from the edge of the serving plate, start sliding the omelet onto the plate.

If the omelet breaks apart, piece it back together, rearrange the toppings or add more cheese to cover patched spots and serve.

Western Way
Bed & Breakfast

13606 Henson Road   P.O. Box 743

Holt, MO 64048   Kearney, MO 64060

(816)628-5686

othehill@flash.net

Hosts: Bill and Connie Green

The Western Way Bed & Breakfast is on a 55-acre horse ranch named Over the Hill Ranch. The Greens have a beautiful log home plus a log guest house with two units in it and one room in the house. Two rooms have Jacuzzi tubs, and there is also a hot tub outside.

Although horseback riding is not allowed, Bill harnesses up their draft horse, Duke, and often gives buggy rides when weather permits. The ranch is very scenic and secluded, making it the perfect romantic hideaway. Connie loves to cook and takes great pride in serving outstanding breakfasts.

Rates at Western Way range from $100-$125.
Rates include a full breakfast.

Apricot Croissants

This is probably the most popular dish served at the Western Way Bed & Breakfast, but this can also be served as a dessert for an evening meal. Peach preserves or orange marmalade can be substituted for apricot preserves, if preferred.

serves 6

6 croissants (preferably cocktail size)
1 1/2 cups apricot preserves
3 ounces frozen concentrate orange juice, thawed and undiluted
5 eggs
1 cup heavy cream
1 teaspoon almond extract

1 small mixing bowl
1 medium mixing bowl
1 9x13 inch baking pan or 6 individual baking dishes
1 pan larger than 9x13 inches to be used as a hot water bath
Baking Time: 30 minutes
Baking Temperature: 350 °

Cut croissants in half lengthwise and place bottoms in buttered pan.

Thin apricot preserves with orange juice concentrate in small bowl and spoon over bottom halves of croissants, saving some for glaze. Replace tops.

Whisk eggs, cream and almond extract in medium bowl and pour over tops of croissants. Spread with remaining glaze.

Cover and let set in refrigerator overnight. Take out 45 minutes before baking. Place pan in larger pan with hot water placed in it and bake approximately 30 minutes until custard is set and croissant is nicely browned on top. The hot water bath, or bain marie, will help the custard cook gently and not curdle and also help keep the cooked dish stay warm. Try to serve immediately if possible.

Garnish with fresh fruit in season, such as kiwi, strawberries or raspberries.

The Parlor
Bed & Breakfast

203 South Knob Street
Ironton, MO 63650
(573)546-2670
www.TheParlorBandB.com
TheParlor@TheParlorBandB.com

Hosts: Jeannette Schrum and Dana Campbell

Our elegant Victorian home was completed in 1908 by a noted architect, Charles J. Tual, as a gift for his bride. Our house has many special effects, from the grand entrance to gingerbread and stained glass windows throughout the house. We have tried to capture the charm and elegance of these ornate times. This is a great place to celebrate *over the hill* birthdays with style or just have a relaxing romantic getaway in the beautiful Arcadia Valley in the Ozark Hills. We have many state parks, quaint stores and antique shops nearby.

In the late 1950s and early 1960s, the house was a funeral parlor, thus the name. To entertain our guests, we have murder mystery dinners and weekends, complete with a 1974 Cadillac hearse. We can help you plan a getaway that special someone will remember always.

Rates at the Parlor range from $75-$95.
Rates include a big country breakfast.

Turtle Brownies

This chocolate delight is like a lot of romantic goodies: it should be stored in a plain brown wrap

serves 12

1 package (14 ounces) caramels
2/3 cup evaporated milk
1 cup margarine, softened
1 cup nuts, walnuts or pecans
12 ounces semi-sweet chocolate chips
1 box (18.5 ounces) German chocolate cake mix

1 large mixing bowl
1 double boiler
1 9x13 inch baking dish
12 dessert plates
Baking Time: 20 minutes
Baking Temperature: 350 °

Combine caramels and 1/3 cup evaporated milk in double boiler; stir mixture until melted.

Combine cake mix, remaining evaporated milk and margarine. Blend until mixture holds together. Stir in nuts.

Press 1/2 of the cake mixture in greased baking dish. Bake at 350 ° for 6 minutes and remove from oven.

Sprinkle chocolate chips on top. Pour melted caramels evenly over top of chips. Crumble remaining mixture over caramels and bake at 350 ° for 15-20 minutes.

Cool slightly and cut into bars.

Huber's Ferry
Bed & Breakfast

HCR 33 Box 159
Jefferson City, MO 65101
(573)455-2979
http://www.bbonline.com/mo/hubersferry/

Hosts: David and Barbara Plummer

Huber's Ferry Bed & Breakfast, which is listed on the National Register of Historic Places, holds a majestic position atop the bluffs overlooking the Osage and Maries Rivers.

Step back to a more peaceful, romantic time. The landscaped grounds attract hummingbirds and butterflies in warmer seasons. The Osage and Maries Rivers are home to bald eagles in the winter months. Binoculars are available to view the eagles and other wildlife. The home is filled with family heirlooms and period antiques. The four bright, airy and spacious guest rooms have private baths, and each has its own special view of the rivers or spacious yard.

After enjoying a full breakfast, a day's activities may include biking on the Katy trail, hiking at Painted Rock State Park, touring the state capitol, visiting local wineries, or shopping in the local antique shops.

Rates at Huber's Ferry range from $80-$90.
Rates include a full breakfast.

Grandmother's Chocolate Cake with Creamy Mocha Cocoa Frosting

Barbara's grandmother always had this cake available. The cake freezes well. Barbara cuts the cake in a h[...] special occasions for guests.

serves 10

1/2 cup butter
1/4 cup vegetable shortening (not oil)
3 Tablespoons unsweetened cocoa powder
1 cup water
2 cups flour
2 cups sugar
2 eggs, slightly beaten
1/2 cup buttermilk
1 Tablespoon baking soda
3/4 teaspoon cinnamon
2 teaspoons vanilla

Frosting:
1/2 cup butter
3 Tablespoons unsweetened cocoa powder
1 teaspoon vanilla
2 Tablespoons strong coffee
2 2/3 cups sifted confectioners' sugar

Chocolate Sauce:
3/4 cup water
1/3 cup honey
3 Tablespoons unsweetened cocoa powder
1 Tablespoon butter
1 teaspoon vanilla

1 medium mixing bowl
1 small saucepan
2 medium saucepans
1 10 1/2 x 15 1/2 inch jelly roll pan
Baking Time: 20 minutes
Baking Temperature: 350 °

In a medium saucepan, bring butter, shortening, cocoa powder and water to a boil. In a medium mixing bowl, combine flour and sugar. Add the liquid cocoa powder mixture to the dry ingredients and mix well. Add eggs, buttermilk, baking soda, cinnamon and vanilla; mix well. Place mixture in greased and floured jelly roll pan.

Bake at 350 ° for 20 minutes or until toothpick comes out clean. Do not overbake. Cool in pan.

Frosting:
Melt butter in medium saucepan. Add cocoa powder, vanilla and coffee; mix well. Stir in confectioners' sugar while mixture is hot. Beat until smooth, glossy and easy to spread. If not glossy, stir in a few drops of hot water or coffee. Frost the cake while the frosting and cake are warm.

Chocolate Sauce:
In a small sauce pan, stir water and honey to combine. Cook over medium heat, without stirring, to syrup stage (about 5 minutes). Add cocoa powder, butter and vanilla; stir.

Serve hot. If made in advance, keep the sauce hot in a double boiler. Drizzle sauce around cake or serving plate and garnish with red berries and mint leaves, if desired.

55

Prosperity School
Bed & Breakfast

4788 County Road 200
Joplin, MO 64801
(417)673-0833
www.joplinbedandbreakfast.com
pwhyte@cstn.net

Hosts: Roy and Pam Whyte

Our schoolhouse was built in 1907 and operated as a school until 1962 when the enrollment had dwindled to 32 students. There was never indoor plumbing, and the original outhouses still stand. The building had fallen into disrepair and was used by local teenagers as a party place. Legend had it that the school was haunted.

We bought the building in 1998 and spent the next 20 months remodeling. We created four luxurious guest rooms, each with a private bath featuring tile showers, a claw foot tub or a whirlpool tub for two. Our guests are encouraged to venture out of their rooms and explore the two acres of landscaped grounds or enjoy our library and collection of movies.

We are conveniently located right outside the city limits of Joplin and Carthage. We are close to Precious Moments, Missouri Southern State College, excellent shopping and a variety of wonderful restaurants. We also host luncheons and dinners for groups by request, small indoor weddings and outdoor weddings.

Rates at Prosperity School range from $85-$105.
Rates include a full breakfast.

Prosperity Apple with Caramel Sauce and Chantilly Cream

We began serving this recipe the first fall that we were open. It has evolved into its present state. Our plan was to return to fresh fruit in the spring, but our guests always request this dish. This is our signature dish.

serves 4

4 apples, peeled and cored
1 Tablespoon cinnamon
water
fresh mint leaves for garnish

Caramel Sauce:
3 Tablespoons butter
3 Tablespoons heavy cream
3 Tablespoons packed brown sugar

Chantilly Cream:
1/2 cup heavy cream
1 Tablespoon powdered sugar
1/4 teaspoon pure vanilla extract

1 small mixing bowl
1 medium saucepan
1 electric mixer

Peel and core apples and place in saucepan. Add water to come about 2/3 of the way up the apple. Add cinnamon. Boil over medium heat until tender, approximately 10 minutes.

Place approximately 1 Tablespoon of caramel sauce in bottom of sherbet dish. Put apple in the center of the sauce and top with Chantilly cream. Garnish with fresh mint leaves.

Caramel Sauce:
Place butter, cream and brown sugar in heavy saucepan. Stirring constantly, bring to a boil and continue cooking for 1 minute. Let stand for 20 minutes.

Chantilly Cream:
Chill bowl and beaters. Put heavy cream in bowl and whip with electric mixer until thickened and peaks will stand. Add powdered sugar and vanilla.

Dome Ridge
Bed & Breakfast

14360 Northwest Walker Road
Kansas City, MO 64164
(816)532-4074
wnfaust@aol.com

Hosts: Roberta and Bill Faust

Dome Ridge is nestled in 17 acres of trees and is a great place for a romantic getaway. We have an outside hot tub or choose the king room with an indoor hot tub. All four rooms have a television, VCR, and our movie library exceeds 600 titles. We have a pool table, board games, BBQ grills, a screened in gazebo and a new sun room. The entire property is non-smoking.

Let Dome Ridge refresh your body and soul in our beautiful nature setting.

Rates at Dome Ridge range from $70-$95.
Rates include a full breakfast.

Sweetheart Frozen Fruit Mold

About six years ago, we were full with the most romantic men bearing flowers around Valentine's Day. I decided to make something to start breakfast that would shout "Valentine". For our couples, I chose to make frozen fruit in a cake pan that made six hearts. It was such a success that I always have it on hand in my freezer.

serves 16

1 can (6 ounces) frozen orange juice, thawed
1 can (6 ounces) frozen lemonade, thawed
2/3 cup sugar
1 carton (16 ounces) frozen sliced strawberries, thawed
1 can (20 ounces) crushed pineapple, not drained
4 large ripe bananas, mashed
1 can (12 ounces) ginger ale

Toppings:
kiwi
strawberries

1 large mixing bowl
1 large spoon
1 6-heart cake pan
6 individual serving dishes

Combine all ingredients in a large mixing bowl. Ladle into freezer safe molds and freeze.

Set molds in warm water to loosen, then put in individual serving dishes.

Let set at room temperature for 25-30 minutes before serving.

Top with a slice of kiwi, then top with a strawberry.

Su Casa
Bed & Breakfast

9004 East 92nd Street
Kansas City, MO 64138
(816)965-5647 or (866)632-2136
www.sucasabb.com
sucasa@kc.rr.com

Host: Lois Hoover

You are welcome to visit this comfortable, spacious ranch home situated on a beautiful five-acre lot at the farthest edge of the city. The simple
beauty of nature, Midwestern hospitality and Southwestern décor combines
with technological conveniences to make your stay the most interesting yet!
Relax in the Jacuzzi, swim in the 18x36 foot in-ground pool, enjoy yourself in
the game room, view a recent movie in the 20-seat in-home theater, enjoy
watching the antics of the resident llamas, goats, horses, ducks and geese, or
just relax in the privacy of your own room watching cable television or reading.

The Southwestern theme blends artwork, furniture, pottery and music
from Mexico, the American West and Native America. Weekend breakfast is a
unique experience at Su Casa because the first guest to arrive chooses breakfast
for the next morning. A breakfast bar including coffee, juice, fresh fruit, yogurt,
cereal and baked goods is available at your convenience on weekdays. Everyone is welcome here. *Mi casa es su casa!*

Rates at Su Casa range from $65-$100.
Rates include a full breakfast on weekends and a breakfast bar on weekdays.

Su Casa's Favorite Crème Brulee French Toast

Su Casa Bed & Breakfast offers a "flexible breakfast menu." Guests can select from each category of fruit, eggs, French toast/pancakes, breakfast breads and meat. The following recipe always entices guests to choose it and, judging from their comments, they love it. Lots of guests have asked for this recipe. The secret to its success is in quality ingredients and its comfort food taste. It is a make-ahead recipe that you will fix again and again!

serves 4-6

1 stick butter
1 cup packed brown sugar
2 Tablespoons corn syrup
1 round loaf King's Hawaiian bread or Challah loaf
5 large eggs
1 1/2 cups half-and-half
1 teaspoon real vanilla
1 Tablespoon Grand Marnier
1/4 teaspoon salt

1 medium mixing bowl
1 small saucepan
1 9x13 inch baking dish
Baking Time: 35-40 minutes
Baking Temperature: 350 °

In small, heavy saucepan, melt butter with brown sugar and corn syrup over moderate heat, stirring until smooth and pour into baking dish.

Cut loaf of bread in half. Starting with center portions, cut 1 inch thick slices, enough to fit closely into baking dish. Trim crusts. Arrange slices into dish, squeezing to fit.

In bowl, whisk together eggs, half-and-half, vanilla, Grand Marnier and salt until well combined. Pour evenly over bread.

Chill bread mixture, covered, for at least 8 hours and up to one day.

Preheat oven to 350 °. Remove dish from refrigerator one hour before baking. Bake uncovered in middle of oven until puffed and edges are pale golden.

When you serve this wonderful dish, turn the portions upside down onto the serving plates. The delicious sauce is on the bottom.

Wenom-Drake House

6055 Fourth Street
P.O. Box 125
Kimmswick, MO 63053-0125
(636)464-1983
www.bbim.org/wenomdrake

Hosts: Abby and Ken Peck

Built in 1877, the Wenom-Drake House is named after its first two owners. John Wenom built the house where he, his wife and seven children lived. In 1918, his descendants sold the house to Fred Drake. Drake added an addition to the house to house overnight guests, but that addition no longer exists. The house has had several owners over the years. Ken and Abby Peck purchased the home in 1992.

Victorian furnishings accentuate the parlor room that features a beautiful Persian rug. The room also features original artwork and a ceramic chess set. The dining room has many unique furnishings, including a 1930s cupboard, a reproduction Webster wood stove and an unusual plate warmer cabinet. Three guest rooms are on the second floor. Each room is uniquely furnished and some have private baths.

Rates at Wenom-Drake House range from $60-80.
Rates include a full breakfast.

Top of Stove Casserole

Pie-shaped servings cut from a heavy iron skillet are well accepted by guests at the Wenom-Drake House. We prepare this dish when 6-8 people will be sitting at our table. Serve with bacon, sausage and buttermilk biscuits. The attractive thing about this casserole, apart from its great flavor, is its complete preparation on top of the stove.

serves 8

5-6 medium cobbler potatoes, peeled, sliced and diced
1/2 cup sweet green pepper, diced
6-7 medium mushrooms, diced
1 cup ham, cut into 1/4-1/2 inch pieces
1/2 teaspoon Grill-In/Grill-Out seasoning by Excalibur™ (Pekin, IL 61554)
or other seasoning
7 large eggs, well beaten
10 ounces sliced or shredded sharp Cheddar cheese
2-3 Tablespoons butter, divided
2 Tablespoons cooking oil
1 Tablespoon finely cut fresh or dried parsley

1 8-inch bowl
1 small plate
1 10-inch Teflon coated fry pan
1 10-inch iron skillet
spatula
table knife

Lightly brown potatoes over medium heat in Teflon fry pan using 1 Tablespoon butter with some cooking oil. Cover until browning occurs, approximately 12-15 minutes.

Transfer browned potatoes to iron skillet rubbed with cooking oil. Add remaining butter for flavor. Cover for a few minutes to keep potatoes hot.

Add peppers, mushrooms and ham, mixing them into the potatoes.

Add seasoning salt and reduce heat slightly. Cover and heat for 5-8 minutes to warm all ingredients.

Add the well beaten eggs and stir them in thoroughly. When eggs have almost set, cover the top of the ingredients with Cheddar cheese. Cover.

When cheese has begun to melt, sprinkle chopped parsley over the cheese and cover again until it has thoroughly melted.

Place skillet on electric griddle set on warm until ready to serve.

Cut into 8 pie-shaped pieces and serve like a piece of pie. Garnish with parsley.

Bass and Baskets

269 Dogwood Road
Lake Ozark, MO 65049
(573)964-5028
www.bassandbaskets.com
innkeeper@bassandbaskets.com

Hosts: Ed and Debbie Franko

Bass and Baskets beckons you to make this Bed & Breakfast "your home at the lake." Designed with your comfort in mind, each guest room features a fireplace, Jacuzzi tub and a deck overlooking the lake. The common areas provide space for small or large groups to watch movies, play games or just have fun. Enjoy relaxing on the spacious decks or at the water's edge. Shop at the outlet mall, golf, fish or enjoy one of the many other activities at beautiful Lake Ozark. Let Bass and Baskets make this "your home at the lake."

Rates at Bass and Baskets are $125.
Rates include a full breakfast.

Fruit Streusel Pizza

Fruit Streusel Pizza is not a streusel or a pizza but a great combination when made with your favorite fruit. It's quick, easy and yummy!

serves 8-12

1 package white cake mix
1 1/4 cup quick cooking oats
1/3 cup butter
1 egg
nonstick cooking spray

1 can (24 ounces) fruit pie filling

Topping:
3/4 cup reserved crumb mixture
3/4 cup chopped nuts
1/4 cup brown sugar
1/4 teaspoon cinnamon

1 medium glass mixing bowl
1 tart or quiche pan
Baking Time: 25-35 minutes
Baking Temperature: 350 °

In medium mixing bowl, combine cake mix, oats and butter. Blend well. Set aside 3/4 cup of crumb mixture for topping. Add egg to the remaining mixture and mix well.

Spray a tart or quiche pan with nonstick cooking spray. Press mixture into pan. Bake at 350 ° for 10-12 minutes.

Spread pie filling over baked crust. Sprinkle with topping mixture. Bake at 350 ° for 15-20 minutes or until lightly browned.

If baked in a pan with removable bottom, Fruit Streusel Pizza can be removed from the pan and served on a lovely cake plate or serving tray.

Topping:
Mix reserved crumb mixture, nuts, sugar and cinnamon to form topping mixture.

Louisiana Guest House Bed & Breakfast

1311 Georgia Street
Louisiana, MO 63353
(573)754-6366 or (888)753-6366

Hosts: Betty Jo and Mett Bryant

The Louisiana Guest House is a charming 100-year-old Cape Cod home along the Great River Road, about an hour from St. Louis and just minutes from historic Hannibal.

Two upstairs bedrooms are decorated with antique beds and handmade quilts. Private baths feature claw foot tubs and luxurious terrycloth robes. You'll enjoy a wine and cheese tray upon arrival and savor a hearty, homemade breakfast each morning.

Enjoy nearby bike paths, hiking, Amish community, fine dining and antique shops. Watch the eagles as they migrate each winter.

Rates at Louisiana Guest House range from $75-$85.
Rates include a full breakfast.

Mushroom Crust Quiche

Serve with breakfast meat, warm muffins, fresh fruit juice and a special blend of coffee.

serves 4-6

1/2 pound fresh mushrooms, coarsely chopped
3 Tablespoons butter
1/2 cup saltine crackers, finely crushed
1/2 cup green onions
2 cups (8 ounces) shredded Jack or Swiss cheese
1 cup large or small curd cottage cheese
3 large eggs
1/2 teaspoon cayenne pepper
1/2 teaspoon paprika
pimento, to taste (optional)

1 large mixing bowl
1 9-inch pie plate
Baking Time: 20-25 minutes
Baking Temperature: 350°

Sauté onions and mushrooms in butter until limp. Stir in crushed saltines. Turn into well greased pie plate. Press mixture firmly over bottom and up sides.

Sprinkle shredded cheese over mushroom crust.

In blender, blend cottage cheese, eggs and cayenne pepper until smooth. Turn into crust; sprinkle with paprika. You can add pimento to mixture at this time.

Bake at 350° for 20-25 minutes, until knife inserted in center comes out clean. Let stand for 10 minutes before cutting.

Garnish with parsley and fresh tomatoes on the side.

St. Agnes Hall
Bed & Breakfast

502 Jackson Street
Macon, MO 63552
(660)385-2774
www.saintagneshall.com
info@saintagneshall.com

Hosts: Scott and Carol Phillips

Since 1986, Carol and Scott have shared their graciously restored historic home, offering genuine hospitality and charming accommodations. St. Agnes Hall is a welcoming getaway—the perfect place to rediscover relaxation! Savor the past as you enjoy the antique décor and casual elegance of "The Hall".

Feel the calmness of a time past…comfort is paramount! Guest rooms with unique personalities have queen accommodations, lots of amenities, private baths and cable TV.

Enjoy a generous breakfast at your leisure in private or join other guests in the sunny dining room. Weather permitting, guests usually choose to linger over breakfast at one of the tables in the garden. The lush gardens with brick walks, cozy decks, vine covered trellis and covered swing "call" to you to enjoy this quiet haven.

This stately old brick house adjacent to Jackson Street has an intriguing history. It was built in the late 1840s on an original land patent by the gentleman hired to survey and plat the city. It was rumored to have been a "safe house" in the years prior to the Civil War when it was commandeered for use as Union headquarters. In 1884, Louisa Smith traveled from Staunton, Virginia, to convert the property into St. Agnes Hall, a boarding and day school for young ladies, which is how it operated until 1895. "The Hall" was remodeled as a private residence by her daughter and son-in-law and was the childhood home of U.S. Senator James Preston Kem. Converted into apartments during World War II, it was home to many young women filling jobs previously held by draftees. After the war, it was home to many newlyweds.

Macon is a great place to come and enjoy a slower pace! Browse in our many antique shops and stores downtown where you can still get a fountain Coke at Miller's Rexall Drug Store, but I suggest you try their famous "Old Maid". Macon has fine restaurants, a triplex cinema and even a drive-in theater, a challenging golf course and lakes for fishing, boating and swimming. There is more to discover, so just come see for yourself!

Rates at St. Agnes Hall range from $78-$98.
Rates include a full breakfast.

Apple-Orange Walnut Bread

A very flavorful bread that is easy to make. It is unusual because you don't peel your apples or orange and that's a real "flavor booster". This moist bread freezes well so you always have a treat ready when friends stop by for coffee.

makes 3 medium size loaves

---

2 large unpeeled baking apples, cored and quartered
1 large unpeeled orange, quartered with seeds removed (I use kitchen
shears to snip across the sections to make it easier to
      take out the seeds)
1 1/2 cups raisins (I like to use golden)
2/3 cup shortening
2 cups white sugar
4 eggs
1 teaspoon lemon extract
4 cups all-purpose flour
2 teaspoons baking powder
1 1/2 teaspoons baking soda
1 teaspoon salt
2/3 cup orange juice
1 cup chopped black walnuts-may substitute pecans

1 medium mixing bowl
1 large mixing bowl
food processor and mixer
3 medium size (4x8x2 1/2) bread pans
Baking Time: 45-55 minutes
Baking Temperature: 350 °

Put apples, orange and raisins in food processor; blend until finely chopped. Set aside.

In a large mixing bowl, cream shortening and sugar. Add eggs, one at a time, beating well with mixer after each addition. Beat until light and fluffy. Add lemon extract and mix.

Combine dry ingredients in a medium mixing bowl; stir to blend. Add dry ingredients to creamed mixture a little at a time, alternating with orange juice. Blend well after each addition. Stir in chopped nuts and fruit mixture.

Pour into 3 greased loaf pans and bake at 350 ° for 45-55 minutes. Let set in pans for 10 minutes before removing. Place on wire rack to cool.

The Dickey House
Bed & Breakfast, Ltd.

331 South Clay Street
Marshfield, MO 65706
(417)468-3000 or (800)450-7444
www.dickeyhouse.com
info@dickeyhouse.com

Hosts: Larry and Michaelene Stevens

The Dickey House is a lovely and gracious Greek Revival Antebellum mansion built at the turn of the century by Samuel Dickey, a prominent prosecuting attorney. It remained in the Dickey family until 1970, and today is AAA Four Diamond rated B&B that has been featured in Time Magazine (October 2000). The house has been host to many famous people, such as William Jennings Bryant, President Bush (the 1st), Governor and Mrs. Carnahan, as well as seven Missouri past senators and governors.

The mansion rests on two acres of manicured lawns and gardens and is framed by ancient oak, hickory and maple trees. You may visit the aviary and enjoy the cooing of doves or sit by the pond watching the Koi and listening to the waterfall. Perhaps you may wish to read your favorite book on the porch, sit in the porch swing or melt your cares away in the hot tub.

Come refresh and relax with us! Allow us to pamper you with homemade goodies, wonderful breakfasts and the perfect romantic getaway! We promise to exceed your expectations!

We are open all year and offer three lovely guest rooms in the mansion and four private and romantic suites on the property. Children 12 and older are welcome. No pets, please. Smoking is only permitted outside.

Rates at the Dickey House range from $65-$145.
Rates include a full breakfast.

Dickey House "No Bake" Valentine's Truffles

These rich, hand-made candies are a favorite of our guests. They are quick and easy to make; however, your guests will think you spent all day preparing them. We make them daily during the month of February and put them in all of our rooms to celebrate Valentine's Day. We suggest you put them in a small heart shaped box tied with red ribbon or put them in a champagne glass. Enjoy! By the way, these freeze exceptionally well. Set them out on a plate for about 30 minutes before you intend to serve them.

makes about 6 dozen

3 cups (18 ounces) semi-sweet chocolate chips
1 can (14 ounces) sweetened condensed milk or creamy chocolate
     sweetened condensed milk (do not use evaporated milk)

choose one or more of the following:
1 Tablespoon pure vanilla extract (do not use imitation vanilla)
         or
1 teaspoon pure vanilla extract (do not use imitation vanilla)
3 drops orange oil
3 drops peppermint oil
3 drops rum extract

Coatings (you can use one...or all)
finely chopped toasted nuts
chocolate sprinkles
unsweetened cocoa powder
tiny hard candies (such as small hearts)
flaked coconut
colored sprinkles
powdered sugar
purchased frosting

1-4 small mixing bowls
1 medium saucepan
Prep Time: approximately 10 minutes, plus shaping and decorating time
Chilling Time: 2-3 hours

Melt the chips with the sweetened condensed milk in a medium saucepan. Remove from heat when chips are melted. Separate mixture into several small bowls (the number of bowls depends on the number of flavorings that you will be using). Stir the flavorings into the mixture; use one flavoring per bowl. Cover and chill for 2-3 hours.

Shape into 1 inch balls. Roll in the desired coating and/or decorate with frosting and candies. Put each truffle in a small paper candy wrapper. Store tightly covered in refrigerator or freeze for future use.

Dickey House Ham & Egg Breakfast Braid

This beautiful, delicious braid is perfect for a late morning brunch or special morning breakfast. It takes about 30 minutes to prepare and 30-35 minutes to bake. Your family and guests will think you spent hours preparing it! Serve it with baked hash browns and fresh fruit.

serves 8-10

2 packages (8 ounces each) refrigerated crescent rolls or your favorite pastry dough
1/4 pound thinly sliced deli ham
1/2 cup (2 ounces) Cheddar cheese, shredded
fresh sliced button or Portobello mushrooms

Filling:
4 ounces cream cheese
1/2 cup milk
8 eggs
1/4 teaspoon salt
dash ground pepper
1/4 cup red bell pepper, chopped
2 Tablespoons sliced green onions with tops
1 teaspoon butter or margarine

2 quart microwave safe bowl
1 10-inch nonstick frying pan
1 12x15 inch cookie sheet
Baking Time: 30-35 minutes
Baking Temperature: 375 °

Filling:
Place cream cheese and milk in bowl. Microwave on high for 1 minute. Whisk until smooth.

Separate 1 egg. Reserve the egg white and add the yolk and the remaining 7 whole eggs, salt and pepper to the cream cheese and milk. Whisk to combine. Add the bell pepper and onions to the mixture.

Melt the butter in a frying pan over medium-low heat. Add the egg mixture and cook, stirring occasionally, until the eggs are set but still moist. Remove pan from heat and set aside.

Preheat oven to 375 °. Unroll 1 package of crescent rolls; do not separate. Arrange longest side of dough across width of cookie sheet. Repeat with remaining package of dough. Roll or pinch dough to seal perforations. On longest sides of pan, cut dough into strips 1 1/2 inches apart and 3 inches deep. There will be 6 inches in the center for the filling.

Arrange the ham evenly over the middle of the dough. Spoon the egg mixture over the ham. Top with mushrooms and one half of the cheese.

To braid, lift strips of dough across filling to meet in the center, twisting each strip to form a braid. Brush the dough lightly with the beaten egg white.

Bake 30-35 minutes or until deep golden brown. Cool for five minutes. Cut into slices and serve.

Another Great Recipe from the Dickey House...

Apple Strudel Waffles

These delicious waffles, served with apple cider syrup, taste just like Grandma's homemade apple strudel. Our guests can't get enough of them! We hope you enjoy them as much as we enjoy making them!

serves 4-6

3 medium Granny Smith apples
1 Tablespoon brown sugar
2 cups Bisquick mix or your own favorite waffle dry mix
1 large egg, beaten
1/2 teaspoon orange peel, grated
1/2 teaspoon lemon peel, grated
1 teaspoon pure vanilla extract (do not use imitation)
3/4 teaspoon cinnamon
3/4-1 cup whole milk
1/4 cup raisins
1/3 cup broken or chopped walnuts

2 glass microwave safe bowls
1 Belgian waffle iron

Preheat the waffle iron. Peel, core and thinly slice apples into bowl. Add the brown sugar and toss lightly. Microwave uncovered on high for 2 minutes. Set aside.

Mix all ingredients except for the raisins and nuts. Add the raisins and nuts when your batter is smooth and all of the flour is moist. Let stand for at least 5 minutes before proceeding to the next step.

Mix batter and pour 1/4-1/3 cup batter into iron. Arrange apple slices on each waffle. Close iron.

Arrange waffles (2 per person) on top of each other, slightly offset. Garnish with whipped cream and a few of the sliced apples. Serve with maple syrup or apple cider syrup.

Variation: Top with a scoop of vanilla ice cream, garnish with apple slices and drizzle with warm syrup.

Apple Cider Syrup:
2 Tablespoons butter
1/4 cup brown sugar
1 cup apple cider or apple juice
1/2 teaspoon cinnamon
1/2 teaspoon cornstarch (optional)

1 medium saucepan

Put all ingredients in saucepan and bring to a boil. Reduce heat and simmer until thick and smooth, approximately 10 minutes. Keep stirring! You may have to add the cornstarch to the mixture if you're in a hurry and want to thicken it quickly.

The Little House,
A Bed & Breakfast

403 Depot Street
mail: 680 Coventry
Marthasville, MO 63357
(636)456-8230
littlehouse1@socket.net

Hosts: Jerry and Rita Hoelscher

Nestled in the midst of the beautiful bottomland farms and the bluffs that overlook the Missouri River, you'll find The Little House. This homey, well-scrubbed, turn-of-the-century two-bedroom Victorian farmhouse is decorated in a casual style with a touch of wicker scattered about. The Little House easily accommodates six guests. It is located on the Katy State Park Hiking and Biking Trail and the Lewis & Clark Trail, and is surrounded by some of Missouri's finest wineries.

During your stay, you may want to relax from the day's activities by catching some sun on the front porch or with a quiet moment in the shade of our towering maple. The fireplaces can bring a special glow to a chilly day or evening. We live nearby so you can make our Little House yours and relax in your home away from home. We've been inspected and approved by the Bed & Breakfast Inns of Missouri and are listed in their 2000 guidebook and in Harry Hagen's "A Complete Guide to Bed & Breakfasts, Guesthouses & Inns of Missouri". We are also included in Brett Dufur's 4th and 5th editions of his "Katy Trail Guidebook". We'll keep the porch light on and the welcome mat out just for you.

Our Little House is air-conditioned, has cable TV, a phone and is very, very private. We are sure you'll enjoy your stay at The Little House.

Rates at The Little House range from $110 for 2 people to $190 for 6 people.
Rates include a continental plus breakfast.

The Little House Orange Pecan Coffee Cake

The nutty aroma and delicious fruit flavor makes this cake a favorite of both family and guests. It is also one of the prettiest coffee cakes I've seen. I sometimes add chopped dried cranberries.

serves 6-8

1 package (16 ounces) pound cake
2 large eggs, slightly beaten
1/4 cup salad oil
2/3 cup orange juice
1 Tablespoon orange juice concentrate, thawed
1 teaspoon orange zest

Streusel:
1/2 cup dark brown sugar, packed
1/4 cup chopped pecans
1 Tablespoon flour
1 teaspoon orange zest
1 teaspoon butter, melted

Icing:
1/2 cup confectioners' sugar
2 1/2 teaspoons orange juice

1 8 ounce mixing bowl
1 16 ounce mixing bowl
1 large mixer bowl
1 tube pan (angel cake)
Baking Time: 35-40 minutes
Baking Temperature: 350 °

Preparation of streusel & icing: Mix together all ingredients until well blended.

Preheat oven to 350 °. Generously grease and lightly flour tube pan. Prepare streusel as described above and set aside.

In large mixing bowl, combine cake mix, orange juice, eggs, zest and oil with mixer at lowest speed until mixture is moistened, scraping bowl periodically. Then beat the mixture at medium speed for 3 minutes. This will make the cake much lighter.

Pour half of the batter into the tube pan, scatter half of the streusel mix on top, then pour the remainder of the batter. Top with remaining streusel mix.

Bake for 35-40 minutes or until an inserted toothpick comes out clean. Cool for 10 minutes, remove from pan and invert on rack to complete cooling.

Drizzle icing on cake after it has completely cooled.

Wooden Horse
Bed & Breakfast

1007 West Sterling Court
Nixa, MO 65714
(417)724-8756
www.bbonline.com
bigoaktree@msn.com

Hosts: Larry and Valeta Hammar

We invite you to 'feel at home' in our City Close/Country Quiet home, with its warm, comfortable atmosphere that is sprinkled with antiques and unique decorating. Everything is private, as you are the only guest at that time. To relieve life's stresses, take time to ponder while relaxing in the charming gazebo in the woodland garden. Later, star gaze from the spa. As you drift off to sound sleep, you will recall the attention to detail that has been part of every aspect of your stay. When you greet the morning, "too much" breakfast will be waiting for your enjoyment. We are seven miles from Springfield's greatest attractions, Bass Pro and Wonders of Wildlife. We are located close enough to Branson to be convenient but away from the congestion. Come "create a memory" with a stay at the Wooden Horse Bed & Breakfast.

Rates at the Wooden Horse are $85 for double occupancy.
Rates include a full breakfast.

Fruit Enchiladas

This is an easy, versatile and tasty fruit presentation. It can be used for tea time as the breakfast fruit or for dessert by using a different garnish. I have written the recipe for apple, but other fruits of your choice can be used.

serves 8

1 can (21 ounces) apple fruit filling or homemade chunky apple filling
8 6-inch flour tortillas
1 teaspoon ground cinnamon
1/4 cup butter or margarine
1/2 cup sugar
1/2 cup firmly packed light brown sugar
1/2 cup water

1 medium saucepan
1 6x10 inch baking pan
individual dessert plates
Standing Time: 30 minutes
Baking Time: 20 minutes
Baking Temperature: 350 °

Lightly grease bottom of baking dish. Lay tortilla flat and spoon fruit filling down the center of each tortilla. Sprinkle evenly with cinnamon. Roll up and place seam side down in baking dish.

In saucepan, bring butter, sugars and water to a boil. Reduce heat and simmer, stirring constantly, for 3 minutes. Pour over rolled enchiladas in baking dish. Let stand for 30 minutes.

Bake for 20 minutes in a 350 ° oven.

To better fit the dessert plates, I cut each roll in half on an angle.

For tea time, garnish with whipped cream and a sprinkle of nutmeg.

For breakfast, garnish with a dollop of sour cream and a sprinkle of pecans or sliced almonds.

For dessert, garnish with a dip of vanilla ice cream and nuts of your choice.

The Inn at Harbour Ridge

6334 Red Barn Road
P.O. Box 496
Osage Beach, MO 65065
(573)302-0411
www.harbourridgeinn.com
info@harbourridgeinn.com

Hosts: Sue and Ron Westenhaver

Your peaceful port on the lake awaits you at The Inn at Harbour Ridge. Furnished casually and decorated for fun—we guarantee you won't find us stuffy! Relax before one of our five fireplaces. Bubble your cares away in one of our "twosome tubbies". We're just moments away from fine dining, shopping, and golfing. Enjoy a full breakfast in your guest room, the dining room or served on the screened porch. We'd love to show you why we're the lake's most inviting Bed & Breakfast.

Rates at The Inn at Harbour Ridge range from $95-$175.
Rates include a full breakfast.

MacIntosh Muffins

These MacIntosh Apple Muffins have become our signature sweet bread for our lake guests. Guys enjoy the regular size while our ladies appreciate the mini bites. Both sizes are filled to the brim with apples, nuts and coconut. I leave the peel on red apples for a bit of color in the muffins. The applesauce in lieu of oil makes them healthier and moist, too. A dense muffin, they freeze and reheat well. Enjoy!

makes 2 dozen regular or 4 dozen mini muffins

1 cup whole wheat flour
2 cups white flour
2 cups sugar
1 1/4 cups non-sweetened applesauce
3 teaspoons vanilla
1 teaspoon baking soda
1 teaspoon salt
1 teaspoon cinnamon
3 eggs
2 cups MacIntosh or Granny Smith apples, chopped
1 cup coconut
1 cup chopped pecans or walnuts
fresh chopped mint (optional)

Topping:
1/3 cup sugar, white or brown
1 Tablespoon ground cinnamon

1 large mixing bowl
2 regular size muffin pans or 4 mini muffin pans
Baking Time: 25 minutes for regular size; 18-20 minutes for mini size
Baking Temperature: 350 °

Preheat oven to 350 °. Mix ingredients together by hand to blend.

Spoon batter into greased muffin pans or use paper muffin cups to line. Fill cups about 2/3 full.

Bake for 25 minutes for regular size muffin or 18-20 minutes for mini muffins. Bake until top is golden brown. Remove from pan immediately.

Topping:
Mix sugar and cinnamon together and sprinkle generously on muffins before baking.

BarnAgain
Bed & Breakfast

904 West Church Street
Ozark, MO 65721
(417)581-2276 or (877)462-2276
www.bbim.org/barnagain
barnbnb@gte.net

Hosts: Mark and Susan Bryant

The cows never had it as good as this in our two converted dairy barns! An oasis conveniently located between Springfield and Branson, BarnAgain is one of the most unique inns around! We invite you to visit—our barn door is open!

Rates at BarnAgain range from $99-$119.
Rates include a full breakfast.

Peaches & Cream Stuffed French Toast

In the words of the Midwest Living Magazine reporter who stayed here recently, this is a "to die for" French toast recipe! Prep time is only 10 minutes or so, but it must be made the night before. Enjoy this BarnAgain original recipe!

serves 2

French bread
cream cheese
fresh or frozen peaches
1/2 cup brown sugar
4 eggs
1 cup milk
1 teaspoon vanilla
1/4 stick butter (not margarine)
1/4 cup maple syrup
cinnamon
powdered sugar

1 medium flat bottom mixing bowl
1 9-inch pie dish
2 plates
Baking Time: 40 minutes
Baking Temperature: 350 °

The night before breakfast:
Cut four 1 inch thick diagonally sliced pieces of French bread. Liberally coat one side of two of the slices with cream cheese. Cover cream cheese with peach slices. Sprinkle brown sugar over peaches. Place remaining slices of bread onto prepared bread to make 2 sandwiches.

In a 9-inch round pie dish, melt butter. Add maple syrup and 1/4 cup brown sugar to the melted butter and mix thoroughly, spreading evenly over the bottom of the pie dish.

In a separate mixing bowl large enough to dunk the sandwiches in, blend eggs, milk and vanilla. Coat the sandwiches in the egg mixture and place in the pie dish. Pour any remaining egg mixture over the sandwiches. Sprinkle with cinnamon, then cover and refrigerate overnight.

In the morning:
Bake covered for 30 minutes at 350 °, then uncover and bake for 10 minutes or until golden brown. Serve immediately drizzled with warm maple syrup and sprinkled with powdered sugar.

Dear's Rest
Bed & Breakfast

1408 Capp Hill Ranch Road
Ozark, MO 65721
(800)588-2262 (LUV 2 BNB)
www.dearsrest.com
stay@dearsrest.com

Hosts: Linda and Allan Schilter

The quiet peace of the surrounding forest draws our guests like bees to honey. Rustic luxury describes the house and furnishings where our guests may relax in the hot tub "under the stars" year round. One can always enjoy the beauty of the stone fireplace, but winter brings cozy, intimate conversations while watching the flames dance before your eyes. Spring and summer are a joy in the wildflower patch while butterflies flutter and songbirds serenade. If you feel adventuresome, take the snorkels provided and explore the pristine Bull Creek where nature beckons you to find our special *swimmin' hole*.

No matter what the season, breakfast is always an event to look forward to! You will be our "only guest" in this Amish built cedar home where privacy is the rule, never the exception.

Rates at Dear's Rest range from $125-$185.
Rates include a full breakfast.

Morning Delight

This fruit dish is very refreshing. It makes an excellent "home from school" snack or fancy "tea time" treat. Prepare days in advance and garnish with pineapple sherbet. Flowers on the serving plate add appeal.

serves 12

1 large can (29 ounces) sliced peaches, cut to bite size
1 large can (20 ounces) crushed pineapple
2 cups fresh or frozen strawberries
1 large can (16 ounces) frozen orange juice concentrate, undiluted
3 bananas, thinly sliced
1 cup sugar or sugar substitute
2 cups 7up

sherbet, pineapple or orange (as a garnish)

1 large mixing bowl
12 3-ounce plastic cups

Cut peaches into bite size pieces. Add remaining ingredients. Freeze in individual serving size cups.

Thaw slightly before serving and garnish with pineapple or orange sherbet.

English Muffins Extraordinaire

This recipe is very tasty and very impressive. My guests always ooh and aah when I place this platter on the table. The compliments don't stop there. They all agree that it's a "keeper"!

serves 4-8

4 English muffins
6 eggs, hard boiled and sliced
1/2 cup sour cream
1/2 cup mayonnaise
4 lean ham slices
4 ounces Swiss cheese, grated
paprika to garnish

1 small mixing bowl
1 medium saucepan
1 cookie sheet
1 skillet

Brown split muffins in butter.

Mix sour cream and mayonnaise.

Boil eggs until they are hard boiled. Cool slightly, peel and slice.

Layer in order:
muffin
ham
sliced eggs
sour cream mixture
cheese

Sprinkle with paprika.

Broil 1-2 minutes until cheese has melted.

Another great recipe from Dear's Rest:

Elegant Pecan Rolls

These cinnamon/pecan rolls are so easy and so delicious that it's almost sinful to make them and take so many compliments!

serves 8

---

1 dozen frozen bread dough balls
1 box (4 ounces) butterscotch pudding (not instant)
1/2 cup brown sugar
1/2 stick butter
1/2 cup chopped pecans
1/2 teaspoon cinnamon

1 small mixing bowl
1 bundt pan
1 cake plate
Baking Time: 20 minutes
Baking Temperature: 350 °

Place frozen bread dough balls in a greased bundt pan.

In mixing bowl, mix rest of ingredients. Microwave for 1 minute, stir and microwave again for 1 minute. Don't overcook!

Drizzle warm mixture over frozen dough.

Let set overnight. I put it in a cold oven.

In the morning, preheat oven to 350 ° and bake for 20 minutes.

Turn out on a pretty cake plate and serve with a flourish!

La Belle Maison
Bed & Breakfast

200 West Broadway
Plattsburg, MO 64477
(816)930-3243
www.labellemaisonbb.com
info@labellemaisonbb.com

Hosts: Phillip and Catherine Martin

La Belle Maison Bed & Breakfast creates a private world where romance and comfort have a decidedly French air. "The Beautiful House" in historic Plattsburg is a peaceful stroll from antiques and specialty shops, restaurants and tree lined streets of old Victorian homes.

Rates at La Belle Maison range from $80-$90.
Rates include a full gourmet breakfast.

Catherine's Baked Pears

A fine dish that is simple but will impress your most regal of guests. Catherine's blend of spices and brown sugar help create a fan fare of tastes. Use this dish for a late evening treat, or compliment a gourmet, savory breakfast with the sweetness of a perfect pear. Bon Appetit!

serves 4

2 medium pears, halved and cored (Bosc or Bartlett)
1/2 cup raisins
1/2 cup chopped pecans
1 cup brown sugar
5 Tablespoons butter
1 cup warm water
cinnamon, nutmeg and whole cloves to taste

1 small mixing bowl
1 9x13 inch baking pan
4 small dessert plates
Baking Time: 45 minutes
Baking Temperature: 350 °

Cut pears in halves and core. Put 1 Tablespoon butter in cored area of each pear. Place face down in baking pan.

In a small bowl, mix all other ingredients. Pour mixture over pears. Cover pan with foil and place in oven for 45 minutes.

When pears become soft, remove to individual plates. Spoon remainder of sauce and goodies onto each pear equally.

Serve hot or warm; don't forget to garnish. Try a strawberry or orange twist with a sprig of mint.

Mulberry Hill
Bed & Breakfast

226 North Armstrong
Pleasant Hill, MO 64080
(816)540-3457
www.mulberryhillbandb.com
mulberryhill@earthlink.net

Hosts: Roy and Pat Keck

The peaceful, relaxing atmosphere at Mulberry Hill is a welcome change from a hectic schedule. This is the perfect place for a romantic getaway, honeymoon or to celebrate a special occasion. There are five lovely guest rooms with private baths, and three of them have Jacuzzi tubs.

We are only 45 minutes from Kansas City. Locally, enjoy antiques, golf, swimming, biking, country music shows or just relaxing.

Rates at Mulberry Hill range from $50-$110.
Rates include a full breakfast.

Spinach Crepes

This tasty crepe can be served as an entrée or a side dish.

makes 16 crepes

8 ounces frozen cut leaf spinach
1/4 cup onion, chopped
1 large clove garlic, minced
16 ounces Ricotta cheese
1/3 cup grated Parmesan cheese
1 teaspoon salt

16 prepared crepes

Sauce:
2 Tablespoons butter
3 Tablespoons flour
1 teaspoon salt
2 cups milk
1/2 cup Parmesan cheese

1 12-inch skillet
1 9x13 baking dish
Baking Time: 20 minutes
Baking Temperature: 350 °

Thaw spinach. Cook spinach, onion, garlic and salt over medium high heat until moisture has evaporated.

Add Ricotta and Parmesan cheeses. Heat thoroughly.

Place 1/3 to 1/2 cup mixture in center of crepe and fold sides of crepe over mixture. Place in baking dish.

Bake in a 350 ° oven for 20 minutes.

The crepes can be frozen until ready to use, then thawed and baked.

Sauce:
Melt butter in skillet. Add flour and salt; stir. Add milk and cook over medium heat until thickened. Add Parmesan cheese and mix well.

Serve 2 or 3 Tablespoons over crepe.

School House
Bed & Breakfast

504 3rd Street
Rocheport, MO 65279
(573)698-2022
www.schoolhousebandb.com
innkeeper@schoolhousebandb.com

Hosts: Vicki Ott and Penny Province

The School House Bed & Breakfast, circa 1914, is listed on the National Historic Register. The inn was once a school for grades 1-12. After a major renovation, the Bed & Breakfast opened in 1988 with 10 distinct guest rooms, each decorated in beautiful antiques, some with Jacuzzis, all with private baths. Located just two blocks from the Katy Trail, the School House is within walking distance to nationally known antique shops, great cafés, and the Les Bourgeois Vineyards and Bistro.

Rates at the School House range from $95-$225.
Rates include a full breakfast.

The Best Chocolate Chip Banana Muffins

This is a very tasty and very easy recipe that always gets rave reviews from my guests. Who can resist a warm chocolaty muffin? They also freeze well, but it's rare to have any left over to freeze.

makes 12 muffins

3 large ripe bananas
3/4 cup sugar
1 egg, lightly beaten
1/3 cup butter, melted
1 1/2 cups all-purpose flour
1 teaspoon baking soda
1 teaspoon baking powder
1/2 teaspoon salt
8 ounces semi-sweet chocolate chips

1 large mixing bowl
1 12-cup muffin pan
Baking Time: 18-20 minutes
Baking Temperature: 375 °

Preheat oven to 375 °. In a large bowl, mash the bananas; add sugar and egg. Add the melted butter, then the flour, baking soda, baking powder and salt. Then stir in the chocolate chips.

Pour the batter into a greased 12-cup muffin pan. Fill each muffin cup about 2/3 full.

Bake for 18-20 minutes until lightly browned and a toothpick inserted in the center comes out clean.

Chewy Chocolate Chip Cookies

These are simply the best chocolate chip cookies—ever! They have become legendary at the School House, with guests begging for the recipe, which I have kept secret…until now.

makes 18 large cookies

2 cups plus 2 Tablespoons all-purpose flour
1/2 teaspoon baking soda
1/2 teaspoon salt
1 1/2 sticks unsalted butter, melted
1 cup dark brown sugar, packed
1/2 cup granulated sugar
1 large egg plus 1 egg yolk
2 teaspoons vanilla extract
1 1/2 cups semi-sweet chocolate chips

2 medium mixing bowls
2 large cookie sheets, parchment lined
Baking Time: 15-18 minutes
Baking Temperature: 325 °

Preheat oven to 325 ° and line cookie sheets with parchment paper.

Whisk flour, baking soda and salt together in medium bowl and set aside.

By hand or with electric mixer, mix butter, sugars and vanilla until blended. Beat in eggs and egg yolk until well combined. Add dry ingredients and beat at low speed until just combined. Stir in chocolate chips.

Roll dough into balls using 1/4 cup dough per ball. Place on cookie sheet, leaving 2 1/2 inches between each ball.

Bake 15-18 minutes until light golden brown. Cool on sheets 10-15 minutes, then peel from parchment paper.

Another great recipe from the School House Bed & Breakfast:

Candied Maple Sausage

This is a fabulous (and fabulously easy) side dish to go with a French toast or pancake entrée. The aroma of the brown sugar bubbling makes the house smell heavenly!

serves 6-8

1 package (12 ounces) maple sausage links
1 cup dark brown sugar, packed
4 Tablespoons yellow mustard

1 large skillet
1 9x13 inch baking pan
Cooking Time: 20-25 minutes

Brown sausage links over medium-high heat until cooked through, approximately 20-25 minutes. Remove from heat and put sausage in baking pan; set aside.

Pour off grease from skillet and return to heat, turning down the temperature to medium. Add brown sugar and mustard and stir until well combined.

Return sausage links to skillet and coat thoroughly with brown sugar mixture.

Serve hot and enjoy!

Yates House
Bed & Breakfast

305 Second Street
PO Box 10
Rocheport, MO 65279
(573)698-2129
www.yateshouse.com
yateshouse@webchoice.net

Hosts: Dixie and Conrad Yates

The Yates House, completed in 1991, is a lovely reproduction of an 1850s roadside inn. The beautiful home is filled with beautiful collections and decorated in exquisite French country and fine Antebellum fabrics and antiques. The main house has three guest rooms. The Yates House is located in the Historic District of Rocheport and is one block from the Katy Trail State Park.

Rates at the Yates House range from $115-$225.
Rates include a full gourmet breakfast.

Confetti Corn Beef Hash

This is a colorful dish—a fun dish for St. Patrick's Day or any other time.

serves 6

2 white boiling potatoes, cut into 1/4 inch dice
6 Tablespoons butter
1 onion, cut into 1/4 inch dice
1 red pepper, cut into 1/4 inch dice
1 green pepper, cut into 1/4 inch dice
1 pound cooked corn beef, cut into 1/4 inch dice
5 Tablespoons chopped parsley
1 teaspoon dried thyme
1 teaspoon coarsely ground black pepper
salt to taste
2 Tablespoons olive oil
6 poached eggs
2 scallions, white bulb and 3 inch green, thinly sliced

1 large mixing bowl
1 small saucepan
1 large skillet
6 serving dishes

Place diced potatoes in a saucepan and cover with cold water. Bring to a boil and simmer until just tender, approximately 10 minutes. Drain and transfer to large bowl. Set aside.

Melt 4 Tablespoons butter in a large skillet. Add onions and red and green peppers. Cook over medium heat until wilted, approximately 5 minutes. Add to potatoes in bowl.

Add corned beef, 4 Tablespoons parsley, thyme, pepper and salt to vegetables. Stir well.

Add remaining 2 Tablespoons of butter and olive oil in skillet. Add hash and spread evenly. Place a heavy plate that is slightly smaller than the skillet over the hash to weigh it down. Cook over medium heat until corned beef has browned slightly, approximately 10 minutes. Remove plate and turn with spatula. Cook until browned.

Divide the hash among 6 plates and top each portion with a poached egg. Sprinkle with scallions and remaining parsley.

Yates House-Garden House
Bed & Breakfast

305 Second Street
PO Box 10
Rocheport, MO 65279
(573)698-2129
www.yateshouse.com
yateshouse@webchoice.net

Hosts: Dixie and Conrad Yates

The Yates House-Garden House is located next door to the Yates House. This 1840s house offers guests three additional rooms to choose from. These spacious rooms, with classic high ceilings, feature the same comfort and elegance as the Yates House. Each room has its own private bath and cable television concealed in an armoire.

Rates at the Yates House-Garden House range from $115-$225.
Rates include a full gourmet breakfast.

Eggs Baked in Dill Crepe Nests

These look like an "art piece" on display and are very tasty. Crepes can be made ahead of time and frozen for up to 3 months or made the day before and refrigerated. Bring to room temperature prior to placing in tins.

serves 4-8

Crepes:
1/2 cup flour
1/8 teaspoon salt
1/8 teaspoon white ground pepper
1/2 cup milk
3 Tablespoons water
1 whole egg
1 egg yolk
1 Tablespoon chopped fresh dill or 1 teaspoon dry dill
1 1/2 Tablespoons butter, melted

Baked Eggs:
8 crepes
8 large eggs
freshly ground pepper
3 Tablespoons butter, melted
8 sprigs of fresh dill for garnish

1 small mixing bowl
1 large mixing bowl
1 crepe pan or 6 inch skillet
1 regular muffin pan
Baking Time: 15-17 minutes total
Baking Temperature: 350 °

In large mixing bowl, combine flour, salt and pepper. Make a well in center of dry ingredients. Combine milk, egg, yolk, butter, water and dill in small bowl; mix to blend. Pour liquid into dry ingredients and mix until well blended. Let batter rest one hour prior to baking.

To prepare crepes, heat crepe pan or skillet over medium-high heat. Stir crepe batter, then ladle 2 Tablespoons batter into pan and swirl to coat surface completely. Let cook until bottom of crepe is lightly browned, approximately 30-45 seconds. Turn and brown other side for 15-20 seconds. Stack between sheets of waxed paper. Continue until all batter is used.

Ease 1 crepe into each of 8 generously buttered standard size muffin tins, gently ruffling the edges. Bake in center of 350 ° oven for 8 minutes.

Break an egg into each crepe cup and season with pepper. Bake for 7-9 minutes or until whites of eggs are set but yolks are still runny. Remove from oven; using both hands, carefully lift crepe cups from muffin tins onto serving plates.

Drizzle about 1 teaspoon of butter over each egg and garnish with dill. Serve immediately.

Boone's Lick Trail Inn

1000 South Main Street
St. Charles, MO 63301
(636)947-7000
www.booneslick.com
info@booneslick.com

Hosts: V'Anne and Paul Mydler

Boone's Lick Trail Inn is an authentic inn in the historic village where Daniel Boone and Lewis and Clark trekked. Explore for yourself this 1840s federal style inn along the wide Missouri River and Katy Trail State Park at the start of the Boone's Lick Trail. The inn is located in the heart of the 12 block National Register Historic District with over 125 shops, 30 restaurants, museums, casinos, river cruise boat and Goldenrod Showboat at our door. This is the only lodging on Main Street of this old river settlement with its brick street, gas lamps and green spaces. V'Anne's delicate lemon biscuits, freshest fruits and hot entrées are served amidst 19th century antiques, compatible reproductions, fragrant flower gardens and Paul's working duck decoy collection. A perfect escape for new inn goers, return guests and corporate guests seeking a different style of lodging. Seasonal duck hunting is available. Located just 8 miles from the St. Louis airport, the inn is only 25 minutes from the sights of St. Louis.

Rates at Boone's Lick Trail Inn range from $115-$175.
Rates include a full breakfast.

Egg and Cheese Ole´ by V'Anne

This is a favorite recipe that our guests love. They like the touch of spiciness that is not overwhelming with the egg mixture. This is an easy mixture when you are in a hurry to serve something special that looks like you worked all morning at it.

serves 15-18

6-8 eggs, beaten
1-2 cups Monterey Jack cheese, shredded
1/2 cup (1 stick) margarine or butter, melted
1 cup skim milk
1/2 to 3/4 cup flour (when baked, its consistency
        should be like a set custard)
1 teaspoon baking powder
1 1/2 cups small curd cottage cheese, drained
1 can (8-10 ounces) chopped tomatoes and green chilies,
        drained (I like Rotel brand)

Topping:
2-3 fresh tomatoes, thinly sliced

1 large mixing bowl
1 9x13 inch Pyrex baking dish
Baking Time: 25-30 minutes
Baking Temperature: 350 °

Combine all ingredients in a large mixing bowl. Mix until well blended.
Pour mixture into buttered Pyrex baking dish. Bake at 350 ° until brown
and puffy and knife test comes out clean.

Place a slice of thinly sliced fresh tomato on each portion before serving.

Egg and cheese ole´ freezes well and can be reheated in the microwave.

Geery's
Bed & Breakfast

720 North Fifth Street
St. Charles, MO 63301
(636)916-5344
www.bedandbreakfast.com/bbc/p609700.asp
pgeerykTj1@aol.com

Hosts: Peter and Marilyn Geery

Our Bed & Breakfast is a turn of the century home located in the historic Frenchtowne District of St. Charles. The interior is decorated in the charm of a quiet time. Here you will find a home dressed with 19th century Scottish antiques, lace and reproductions designed to place you back into a world of cozy romance, coupled with warm, inviting hospitality and a full English breakfast. Each of the three rooms has its own distinct personality: Alexander, Roselea and Lindsay rooms.

Spice up your romance with a fantastic breakfast at Geery's B&B. With the aroma of muffins baking, it's heaven on earth. Forget the calories, forget the cholesterol and chores. RELAX. Enjoy the newspaper or magazine or go for a walk. REKINDLE. Any day can be filled with a few transitions: jazz for rock and roll, classical for hard rock, rest for hustle and bustle.

Rates at Geery's range from $80-$125.
Rates include a full English breakfast.

Fresh Fruit Salad with Honey and Cardamom

Remember that first kiss? Try another. This feast will be ready in minutes. Let the fresh smell of fruit tickle your nose while you savor the taste.

serves 4-6

1/4 cantaloupe, cubed
1/4 honeydew melon, cubed
1/2 apple, cubed
1 cup grapes
Variations:
1 kiwi
5-6 strawberries
1 banana
1 pear

1 medium mixing bowl
4-6 fruit bowls

Wash cantaloupe, honeydew melon and apple; cut away rind/peel.

Place the cubed fruit in medium mixing bowl and add grapes. Mix well. Place in fruit dishes.

Sauce:
1/4 cup honey
1/2 teaspoon ground cardamom

Warm in the microwave for 15 seconds on high. Stir. Pour over the fruit combo and mix.

Serve chilled or warm.

.

Old Elm Tree Inn

1717 Elm Street
St. Charles, MO 63301
(636)947-4843
www.oldelmtreeinn.com
oldelminn@yahoo.com

Host: Martha Kooyumjian

This lovely Victorian home was built in 1904. Completely remodeled, it has many extras. All rooms have private baths, whirlpool tubs, fireplaces, cable TV, refrigerators and telephones. There are also four common rooms on the main floor and a beautiful perennial garden for guests to enjoy. Located 10 blocks from historic Main Street, guests can enjoy great shopping and dining. A three course gourmet breakfast is served in the morning.

Rates at Old Elm Tree Inn range from $95-$130.
Rates include a three course gourmet breakfast.

Ginger Pancakes with Homemade Lemon Sauce

The spices in the pancake batter are a wonderful compliment to the lemon sauce. The pancakes can be made in any size. I like to make them about 7 inches across—remember to make them thin.

serves 6

2 cups pancake mix
1 teaspoon cinnamon
1 teaspoon ground cloves
1/2 teaspoon ground ginger
1 egg
1 1/2 cups 2 percent milk
8 ounces cream cheese, softened in a microwave for 1 minute
nonstick cooking spray

Lemon Sauce:
1 cup butter, melted
2 eggs, well beaten
2 cups sugar
peel of 1 lemon cut into small julienne strips (I like to cook these
        in a microwave to make them soft)
1/2 cup water
6 Tablespoons lemon juice

1 small mixing bowl
1 medium mixing bowl
1 small saucepan
1 electric skillet
1 casserole dish

Mix first 6 ingredients together until smooth with electric mixer. Spray nonstick cooking spray in skillet to grill pancakes. Cook pancakes one at a time over medium high heat. After pouring the batter into the skillet, rotate the skillet to spread the batter. This will make a thinner pancake.

Remove each pancake from the skillet and while it is still hot, place an appropriate amount of softened cream cheese at one end and roll the pancake to resemble a crepe. Place in a casserole dish in a 200 ° holding oven until all the pancakes are done.

Lemon Sauce:
Mix all ingredients together and pour into a saucepan. Bring to a boil. Boil mixture for 2 minutes, stirring constantly.

Victorian Memories
Bed & Breakfast

709 North Fourth Street
St. Charles, MO 63301
(636)940-8111
www.victorianmemories.com
Terrie@victorianmemories.com

Host: Terrie O'Neal

    As you stroll up the ivy edged path of this 1857 Italianate home, you'll feel you have stepped back in time to when life was simple, relaxing and friendly. Pamper yourself with a relaxing soak in one of three whirlpool tubs. Each themed room offers a private bath, cozy fireplace and queen size bed. Let us pamper you Victorian style!

Rates at Victorian Memories range from $129-$169.
Rates include a full breakfast.

Amaretto Grapefruit

A great way to serve this nutritious fruit on a cold winter's day. Some people who do not like cold grapefruit love it warm.

serves 6

3 large grapefruit
6 Tablespoons brown sugar
6 Tablespoons amaretto
6 small dollops vanilla yogurt or whipped cream
cinnamon to taste
sugar to taste

1 round glass dish
6 serving bowls
Baking Time: 10 minutes
Baking Temperature: 345 ° and broil

Wash, cut in half and section grapefruit for easier dining. Preheat oven to 345 °.

Sprinkle each half with 1 Tablespoon brown sugar and 1 Tablespoon amaretto. Place in oven for 10 minutes.

Place under broiler for last few minutes, until sugar melts and top gets crusty.

Top with dollop of yogurt or whipped cream. Sprinkle with cinnamon and sugar to taste.

Serve immediately.

The Mansion at Elfindale
Bed & Breakfast

1701 South Fort
Springfield, MO 65807
(417)831-5400 or (800)443-0237
www.gomansion.com
mansion@cwoc.org

Host: Twyla Nistendirk

The Mansion at Elfindale is one of Missouri's largest bed & breakfasts. It is nestled among trees near a creek in a serene setting. As you enter our spacious foyer with 14 foot tin ceilings, you step back into a Victorian era of yesteryear.

The 3 story graystone building was built in 1892 and was originally a private dwelling. In 1904, the Sisters of Visitation purchased the property and started a private boarding school for girls. The nuns sold the property in 1977, and in 1992, the Elfindale was converted to a bed & breakfast.

The mansion has 13 suites which are tastefully decorated in an old world motif. The suites each have private baths and are furnished in the turn of the century style. The dining room on the main floor will accommodate 60-70 people, and there are two other rooms on the main floor. All three rooms are being used for wedding receptions, banquets, luncheons, dinners, showers, private parties and small weddings. The Chapel at Elfindale, which adjoins the mansion, is also the scene of many weddings. The grounds around the buildings are ablaze with seasonal flowers.

Rates at the Mansion at Elfindale range from $85-$135.
Rates include a full breakfast.

Sweet Potato Pancakes

Serve these tasty pancakes with syrup or top with your favorite pie filling. Yum, yum!

serves 4-6

1 can (15 ounces) sweet potatoes or yams
3 cups pancake mix
2 eggs
2 cups milk, add more if necessary

1 medium mixing bowl
1 griddle

Puree sweet potatoes in mixing bowl.

Add eggs, pancake mix and milk to desired consistency.

Pour 1/3 cup batter onto well greased griddle. Cook until golden brown on each side.

Serve warm with your favorite topping or syrup.

Walnut Street Inn

900 East Walnut Street
Springfield, MO 65806
(417)864-6346
www.walnutstreetinn.com
stay@walnutstreetinn.com

Hosts: Gary and Paula Blankenship

Located in the heart of Springfield's historic district, the Walnut Street Inn has been named one of the "Top Twelve Inns in the Country" by *Country Living* magazine and has also been featured in *Southern Living* magazine. Relax for a while on our front porch swing, the site of countless marriage proposals, and enjoy the natural beauty of the Ozarks. Then sink into a luxurious whirlpool bathtub or curl up with your favorite book in front of your own private fireplace. Whether you are planning your next business trip or your next romantic getaway, this 14-room luxury urban inn is sure to be a perfect fit!

Rates at Walnut Street Inn range from $89-$169.
Rates include a full breakfast.

Sweet Cheese Blintz Soufflés

"When planning a surprise birthday party for my mom at the Walnut Street Inn, this was my request for breakfast. A creamy soufflé that melts in your mouth—perfected with a berry sauce topping in the summer or apple butter in the winter. What better way to show my mum how sweet she is to me."
Triesa, Manager

serves 8

Cake Batter:
1/2 cup butter, softened
1/2 cup sugar
6 eggs
4 teaspoons lemon zest
juice from one lemon
1 cup flour
2 teaspoons baking powder

Filling:
8 ounces cream cheese, softened
2 cups cottage cheese
2 eggs
2 Tablespoons sugar
1 teaspoon vanilla extract

1 medium mixing bowl
Cuisinart food processor
8 4-ounce soufflé dishes
Baking Time: 20-30 minutes
Baking Temperature: 350 °

Spray soufflé cups with nonstick cooking spray. In food processor, combine first 7 ingredients; blend until smooth, then place in bowl.

In food processor, combine filling ingredients and blend until smooth.

Scoop 1/4 cup cake batter into each cup. Top with 1/4 cup filling; then cover with 1/4 cup cake batter.

Bake for 20-30 minutes at 350 ° until puffed and lightly browned on top.

Ham and Cheese Puffs

Puffs have become such a favorite at the Walnut Street Inn that our employees fight over the early shift when Rita is serving them for breakfast. With a flaky crust and great height, they create a picture wonderful enough to eat!

serves 8

1 box (2 sheets) frozen puff pastry, thawed (Pepperidge Farm)
1 pound deli ham, shaved thin
4 ounces Cheddar cheese, grated
1/4 cup sour cream
1 teaspoon dried dill weed or 1 Tablespoon fresh dill
1 egg for egg wash

1 small mixing bowl
1/2 size sheet pan with sides
parchment paper to cover pan
Baking Time: 20-25 minutes
Baking Temperature: 400 °

Combine sour cream and dill; set aside. If your ham is very moist, it is best to spread it out on a sheet pan covered with paper towels and put it in a 350 ° oven for 10-15 minutes to dry it.

Roll out the puff pastry sheets to the size of your sheet pan. Place one pastry sheet on pan and spread the sour cream mixture on the pastry, leaving a 1 inch border for sealing.

Arrange the ham over the sour cream and sprinkle the cheese over the ham. Beat the egg in a small bowl and brush the edges of the pastry before placing the second pastry sheet on top.

Seal the edges with a fork or decorative tool. Brush the top with the egg wash and poke holes or cut slits in the pastry for steam to escape. Small canapés cutters are good for this.

Bake 20-25 minutes at 400 °.

Another Great Recipe from the Walnut Street Inn:

Lavender Bath Salts

There is no better ending to any day than sinking into a luxurious whirlpool bathtub filled with lavender-scented water. Relax your worries away with our recipe for a stress-free evening!

This is a recipe for the body and soul.

This recipe is inedible—Please do not eat it!

1 box Epsom salt
1 box sea salt
1 box borax
1 small box baking soda
10 drops lavender oil

Mix all ingredients.

Store in a cool, dry place.

Painted Lady
Bed & Breakfast

1127 South Jefferson
St. James, MO 65559
(573)265-5008
www.paintedladybandb.com
srzinn@tigernet.missouri.org

Hosts: Sandy and Wanda Zinn

Painted Lady Bed & Breakfast is a Victorian dollhouse decorated throughout with wallpaper and lace. Chandeliers, antiques and art add to its country Victorian charm. In-room Jacuzzis, hot tub, and queen and king size iron and brass beds promise a great night's sleep! In St. James, you will find wineries and the beautiful Meramec Spring Park.

Upon arrival, you'll be treated to a beverage of your choice, treats and a tour of the home. Luxury amenities, nightly turndowns and chocolates await you. You will awaken in the morning to the wonderful aroma of early coffee and a full country breakfast in the making. There are common areas to share with other guests, and the kitchen is always open.

We put great emphasis on cleanliness, comfortable beds and hospitality. We love sharing our home. Our guests come from all walks of life. We want you to enjoy your stay with us and return home safely, feeling pampered, relaxed, and as if you had stayed with family and friends.

Rates at Painted Lady range from $90-$175.
Rates include a full breakfast.

Raisin Bran Muffins

I have shared this recipe with many guests. It's a favorite, and you can make as few or as many as you like—the batter will keep for 5 weeks in the refrigerator.

makes 5 dozen muffins

5 cups sifted flour
3 cups sugar
5 1/2 cups raisin bran
5 teaspoons baking soda
2 teaspoons salt
2 teaspoons cinnamon
4 eggs, beaten
1 quart (4 cups) buttermilk
1 cup oil
2 cups raisins (may use white raisins)

1 large mixing bowl
1 12-cup muffin pan
Baking Time: 20 minutes
Baking Temperature: 350 °

Preheat oven to 350 °.

In large mixing bowl, mix dry ingredients together.

Add eggs, buttermilk and oil to dry mixture; do not overmix.

Add raisins.

Fill greased or lined muffin cups about 2/3 full. Bake for 20 minutes or until tops are a golden brown.

Eastlake Inn
Bed & Breakfast

703 North Kirkwood Road
St. Louis, MO 63122-2719
(314)965-0066
www.eastlakeinn.com
info@eastlakeinn.com

Hosts: Dean and Lori Murray

Eastlake Inn Bed & Breakfast is a 1920 colonial inn located on one acre in historic Kirkwood in west St. Louis County. Beautiful 100-year-old catalpa trees and perennial gardens adorn the grounds for guests to relax in. Our luxury suite has a romantic fireplace in the room. The dream bathroom has a two-person Jacuzzi and double shower. The inn has three rooms and a full gourmet breakfast. Come to St. Louis and see the Arch, botanical gardens and wonderful museums.

Rates at Eastlake Inn range from $75-$200.
Rates include a full breakfast.

Murray's Christmas Lamb Stew

This traditional English recipe was passed down from the McWilliams family to the Murray family and became the traditional Christmas morning breakfast. Suzanne McWilliams Murray lovingly passed this family recipe down to me (her daughter-in-law). This recipe can be made ahead of time, frozen and warmed for your Christmas morning delight or other special occasion. Serve over toasted English muffins or melba toast.

serves 6

3 pounds lamb kidneys (pre-order from your butcher)
4 Tablespoons butter
1 large onion, diced
4 or 5 cups water
1 beef bouillon cube
1/2 lemon, juice only
2-3 Tablespoons flour
1 cup mushrooms, sliced

1 deep stove-top pot
Simmering Time: 45 minutes

Remove white vein from lamb kidney. It is best if the kidneys are partially frozen. Chop kidneys into small 1/2 inch pieces.

In large pot, sauté chopped onion in butter. Add kidneys to the onion. Sauté until kidneys are brown. Cover kidneys with water and add beef bouillon. Simmer 45 minutes.

Add mushrooms and lemon juice. Separate kidneys from juice. Add flour to juice and thicken slightly. Return kidneys to juice.

Spoon over toasted English muffins.

Napoleon's Retreat

1815 Lafayette Avenue
St. Louis, MO 63104
(800)700-9980
www.napoleonsretreat.com
info@napoleonsretreat.com

Hosts: Jeff Archuleta and Michael Lance

Napoleon's Retreat is located in Lafayette Square, which is St. Louis's first historic district and contains the largest collection of Victorian-era architecture in the nation. *Better Homes and Gardens* and *Architecture* magazines have chosen Lafayette Square as one of the "ten prettiest painted places" in the country. Napoleon's Retreat was thus named when Napoleon I, consul of the French Republic when the Louisiana territory was sold to the U.S., "retreated" from the battle of Waterloo.

The inn features four guest rooms and a carriage house suite. Each room is decorated with period antiques and reproduction pieces and features private baths, cable TV and private telephones. A full breakfast is served in the dining room or the courtyard, weather permitting. Be sure to include a walk through Lafayette Park, the oldest city park west of the Mississippi, in your plans.

Rates at Napoleon's Retreat range from $85-$125.
Rates include a full breakfast.

Lemon Currant Scones

makes 8-10 scones

2 cups all-purpose flour
1/2 cup sugar
2 teaspoons baking powder
zest of one lemon
6 Tablespoons (about 3/4 stick) <u>cold</u> butter
1/2 cup currants
1/2 cup cream or half-and-half
1 egg
juice from one lemon
1 beaten egg or milk for wash before baking

1 large mixing bowl
1 baking sheet
Baking Time: 15 minutes
Baking Temperature: 350 °

Combine flour, sugar and baking powder in bowl. Add lemon zest and mix well. Cut butter into small pieces and mix into the dry ingredients by hand until mixture is crumbly. Stir in currants. Beat cream and egg and add to dry ingredients, along with lemon juice, stirring lightly; do not overmix.

Turn mixture onto a lightly floured surface and form into a circle about 3/4 inch thick. Cut into 8-10 triangles, depending on desired size. Place on a lightly greased baking sheet and brush with the beaten egg or milk. Bake at 350 ° for about 15 minutes or until golden brown.

Dr. Hertich's House

99 North Main Street
Ste. Genevieve, MO 63670
(573)883-5744
http://www.bbhost.com/drhertich
Buffin@msn.com

Hosts: Mark and Connie Smith; Janet Joggerst

Although this home was built for a physician in 1850, its amazing suites are definitely for those wanting to be spoiled by the newest generation of luxury amenities. With over 20 jets, waterfall and aromatherapy, the double whirlpool tubs found in your private bath will soak your cares away! When not in the tub, slip on a plush robe and cuddle in the king size bed while enjoying the suite's fireplace. A kitchenette supplied with snacks and drinks, the VCR/cable television and breakfast served en suite are a few of the reasons so many guests return again and again.

Ste. Genevieve is the most historical town in Missouri, being founded in the late 1730s. Not only are there wonderful museums, but boutiques, antique stores, restaurants, hiking, biking and golf are all close by…most within walking distance from the inn. A fabulous setting for a relaxing getaway.

Rates at Dr. Hertich's House range from $179-$189.
Rates include a full breakfast served en suite with
choice of entrées.

Stuffed French Toast with Strawberry Glaze

The combined culinary skills of Connie and Janet gave birth to the inn's "signature dish". Guests assume the recipe is highly difficult due to its fabulous presentation, taste and texture; however, it's one of our easiest (and most requested) recipes!

makes 4 large servings

3 large eggs
1 teaspoon vanilla
3 Tablespoons milk
1 loaf French bread
2 cups corn flakes, crushed
4 Tablespoons margarine for pan frying
       (approximately 1 Tablespoon per slice)

Garnishes:
parsley
strawberries
powdered sugar

Filling:
4 ounces cream cheese, softened
1/4 cup crushed pecans

Sauce:
8 ounces strawberry preserves
1/4 cup orange juice

2 small (2 cup) mixing bowls
2 medium (3 cup) mixing bowls
2 large (12 inch) frying pans
4 dinner plates

Cut French bread into 2 inch slices. Make a pocket in the center of each piece by slicing the bread 3/4 through. Fill the pocket with filling mixture, using 1/8 of prepared filling per slice of bread. Set aside.

Beat eggs, milk and vanilla until well mixed, using medium bowl. Set aside.

Dip bread into egg mixture; roll in corn flakes until well coated. Pan fry in margarine on medium-high heat for 2 1/2 minutes on each side or until light brown.

Place 2 grilled toasts on each plate. Cover with warm preserve mixture. Sprinkle with powdered sugar. Garnish with parsley and fresh sliced strawberries.

Filling:
Combine cream cheese and pecans in small bowl.

Sauce:
Combine preserves with orange juice, stirring until smooth. Heat in microwave 20-30 seconds, until warm. Sauce will be runny.

Southern Hotel

146 South Third Street
Ste. Genevieve, MO 63670
(800)275-1412
www.southernhotelbb.com
mike@southernhotelbb.com

Hosts: Mike, Barbara and Michael Hankins

This graceful 1790s Federal building operated as a hotel from 1805 and was known for the finest accommodations between Natchez and St. Louis. Each of the eight romantic guest rooms contains a collection of country Victorian antiques and delightful "whimsies." Here the past is carefully blended with modern comforts to make your stay a very special experience. The hotel has the first pool hall west of the Mississippi. Each room has a private bath with ball and claw foot hand painted tubs. It was named "One of the Ten Best Inns in the Midwest" by *Midwest Living* magazine and voted one of the 15 "Most Romantic Inns" for 2002 by inn-goers in the U.S. The Southern Hotel is the oldest, longest operating hotel or lodging in the United States west of the Mississippi.

Rates at the Southern Hotel range from $98-$138.
Rates include a full breakfast.

Chutney Cheese Pâte'

This also makes a wonderful sauce. Melt it gently in a microwave on defrost, stirring often. Drape over omelets, chicken or ham crepes, or on hash browns.

makes 1 cup

3 ounces cream cheese, room temperature
1/2 cup shredded Cheddar cheese
2 teaspoons dry sherry
1/4 teaspoon curry powder
1/8 teaspoon salt
1 jar (1/2 cup) Major Greys Chutney

1 medium mixing bowl
1 mixer

Combine all ingredients but Chutney and beat until smooth.

Spread into a 1/2-inch thick circle on a decorative plate.

Chill until firm, at least two hours.

Spread 1/2 cup Chutney on top of mixture.

Garnish with chopped green onions and serve with crackers or brown bread slices.

Brawley Creek
Bed & Breakast

631 Southwest 51ˢᵗ Road
Warrensburg, MO 64093
(660)747-7027 or (800)330-9003
www.bbim.org/brawleycreek
brawleyc@iland.net

Hosts: Regina and John Hess

Brawley Creek Bed & Breakfast is a lodge-like structure amidst a peaceful, wooded sanctuary and has the distinction of being the only Missouri B&B certified as a National Wildlife Federation habitat. We built the inn to provide a secluded 20 acre retreat for those seeking solitude or simply the serenity of the countryside. The inn is situated only 50 feet from Brawley Creek, which runs the length of the property and can be enjoyed from an expansive wrap-around porch. A mile of trails is maintained so that the creek, woods and fields, and frog pond can be experienced directly.

We live simply and attempt to have our lives mesh with the seasons and the tranquility of the forest. Our view is echoed in a notice posted in a favorite Audubon sanctuary: "This is a wooded valley where nothing ever happens, where people simply live, where there is sun and slow peacefulness of day following day. Walk gently…and may some of its peace be yours."

Our highest ambition is that this peacefulness will speak to our guests while they are here and that they will renew a connection with the natural world that they can carry with them when they leave.

Rates at Brawley Creek range from $100-$125.
Rates include a full gourmet breakfast.

Glazed Poppy Seed Bread

Of all the recipes that I treasure most, this is the one! A dear friend shared this with me, and it has made me most beloved with everyone who has ever eaten it. It takes only a few moments to stir everything together, and the recipe can easily be halved to make one loaf or muffins. I always make a second loaf to share with friends or to put in the freezer for those unexpected guests. It is an especially lovely baked gift to give during the winter holidays. Our guests are greeted with thick slices of this delicacy on the table when they come down to breakfast, which also includes papaya halves with sweet lime filling, sage sausage and mushroom quiche, and apple French toast with homemade spiced apple syrup.

makes 2 loaves

3 cups unbleached, all-purpose flour
1 1/2 teaspoons salt
1 1/2 teaspoons baking soda
2 1/2 cups sugar
1 cup butter or margarine with at least 70% vegetable oil
1 1/2 cups milk (I use skim)
1 1/2 Tablespoons poppy seeds
3 eggs
1 1/2 teaspoons pure vanilla extract
1 1/2 teaspoons pure almond extract

Glaze:
3/4 cup sugar
1/4 cup fresh squeezed orange juice
2 Tablespoons butter, melted
1/2 teaspoon pure vanilla extract
1/2 teaspoon pure almond extract

1 large (8 cup) mixing bowl (for bread)
1 small mixing bowl (for glaze)
2 loaf pans (8 1/2 x 4 1/2 x 2 1/2)
Baking Time: 75-85 minutes
            25-30 minutes for 12 muffins
Baking Temperature: 350 °

Place all ingredients in a large mixing bowl. Beat with a mixer for 2 minutes. Dividing batter evenly, pour into 2 loaf pans which have been sprayed with nonstick cooking spray.

Bake at 350 ° for approximately 1 hour 15 minutes. Loaves are done when cracked centers are dry and bread is a deep golden brown.

Remove from oven and immediately cover with glaze. Do not remove from pans.

Glaze:
While bread is baking, combine all ingredients in a small mixing bowl. Microwave on high for 20-25 seconds or until butter is melted. Mix together well. Be sure to stir and reheat, if necessary, before pouring onto loaves.

Pour an even amount of glaze over the hot loaves. Allow the glaze to soak into the loaves for several hours, or for best results, overnight. If soaking overnight, be sure to cover with foil or place in an airtight container when loaves are cool.

Loaves store well in an airtight container for 1 week, and they freeze well for several months.

The Camel Crossing

210 East Gay Street
Warrensburg, MO 64093
(660)429-2973
www.bbim.org/camelx/index.html
camelx@iland.net

Hosts: Ed and Joyce Barnes

The Camel Crossing was built in 1906 and features hardwood floors, fireplaces, pocket doors and spacious entryways. The décor is a mix of east and west. We lived in Saudi Arabia for eight years (former Aramcons). We collected oriental/hand tied carpets, brass and copper pieces, and other artifacts that give the main floor a museum like atmosphere. The second floor has three bedrooms and a lounge; the downstairs area is always available. Guests are welcome to relax on our deck and front porch.

The Camel Crossing is centrally located four blocks from the college and five blocks from the Amtrak depot in Warrensburg. For your convenience, we will pick you up at the Amtrak depot. We are located 45 miles east of Kansas City on Highway 50.

Rates at the Camel Crossing range from $70-$90.
Rates include a full breakfast.

Creamy Baked Chicken Breasts

This dish can be prepared a day ahead of time and is always a hit with our guests. It serves nicely with a green salad, Copper Penny Carrots and Potato Casserole. Bon appetit!

serves 8

8 boneless, skinless chicken breasts halves
8 slices (approx. 1 ounce each) Swiss cheese
1 can (10 3/4 ounces) condensed cream of chicken soup
1/4 cup dry white wine or water
2 cups One Step stuffing mix
1/3 cup butter, melted

1 small mixing bowl
1 9x13 inch baking dish
Baking Time: 50-55 minutes
Baking Temperature: 350 °

Arrange chicken breasts in baking dish that has been sprayed with nonstick cooking spray. Top each piece with a slice of Swiss cheese.

In a small bowl, stir together soup and wine. Spoon evenly over chicken. Sprinkle stuffing mix over sauce. Drizzle evenly with butter.

Bake in a 350 ° oven for 50-55 minutes or until done.

The Good House
Bed & Breakfast

707 North Holden Street
Warrensburg, MO 64093-1127
(660)747-9563
goodhous@iland.net

Host: Nita Good

Multiple seating areas give a pastoral setting to this Victorian mansion, inside and out. This elegant 1903 home features a beautiful golden oak staircase and fireplace. Sitting porches and a brick patio surrounded by beautiful gardens allow guests to enjoy the fully landscaped grounds and mature oak trees. Rooms feature queen size beds and private bathrooms plus central air conditioning on the ground floor and individually controlled A/C upstairs. There are TV/VCRs in the common areas. Ample off-street, lighted parking is available.

The Good House is conveniently located near Central Missouri State University, Powell Gardens, Lake of the Ozarks and Whiteman Air Force Base. Golf courses, shopping, antiques and historical sites are near.

Come, relax under our majestic oaks.

Rates at the Good House are $75.
Rates include a full country breakfast.

Chocolate Éclair Cake

This is such an easy dessert that tastes so good it is worth the 48 hour wait. It really does taste like an éclair without any last minute bother.

serves 12-16

24 graham crackers
2 packages instant French vanilla pudding
3 cups milk
1 carton (9 ounces) Cool Whip, thawed

Topping:
2 ounces unsweetened chocolate, melted
3 Tablespoons butter, melted
1 Tablespoon white corn syrup
3 Tablespoons milk
1 teaspoon vanilla
1 1/2 cups powdered sugar

1 medium mixing bowl
1 9x13 inch pan

Grease a 9x13 inch pan. Line bottom of pan completely with whole graham crackers. Break crackers if needed for edges. Beat pudding and milk together, then fold in thawed Cool Whip.

Layers: crackers, pudding mixture, another layer of crackers and another layer of pudding mixture.

Topping:
Beat well the chocolate, butter, corn syrup, milk and vanilla. Fold in powdered sugar.

Drizzle the topping on the second layer of pudding.

Leave *uncovered* in refrigerator for two days.

Old Drum Inn

315 East Gay Street
Warrensburg, MO 64093-1951
(660)422-8334
www.olddruminn.com
olddrum@iland.net

Hosts: Heidi and Roger Gauert

An Empire home built in 1910, the Old Drum Inn is filled with elegant antiques. In this beautiful home, Heidi and Roger have created a casual, make-yourself-at-home atmosphere. Cozy up with a book from the library and your evening dessert, visit with other guests by the fire, nap in the hammock, roast marshmallows in the patio fireplace under the stars, or rock your cares away on the front porch. A very comfortable bed will lull you to sleep, and a full heartland breakfast will entice you out of bed each morning. We are located near CMSU, Amtrak, antiques and wineries. A nice stopover between Kansas City and St. Louis.

Rates at Old Drum Inn range from $85-$98.
Rates include a full heartland breakfast.

Eggs in a Snow Bank

A lighter eye-popping dish. Great for a travel day when you don't want a heavy meal to weigh you down.

serves 4

4 slices bread
4 thick slices ham
4 slices Swiss cheese
4 eggs, separated

1 medium mixing bowl
1 cookie sheet
Baking Time: 10 minutes
Baking Temperature: 350 °

Lightly toast bread. Place on cookie sheet.

Top each slice of bread with a slice of ham.

Top each slice of bread with a slice of cheese.

Beat egg whites in mixing bowl with electric mixer until fluffy.

Mound egg whites attractively on each slice of bread, leaving a well in the center.

Slide an egg yolk into each well of egg whites.

Bake for 10 minutes in a 350 ° oven and serve.

Victorian Garden Inn

214 East Jackson Street
P.O. Box 1806
Warsaw, MO 65355
(660)438-3005
www.victorian-garden-bandb.com
vgi@ozarks.net

Hosts: Patti Downs and Henry Starcher

The Victorian Garden Inn is a 1908 Queen Anne Victorian house, painted in San Francisco "Painted Lady" style. The house was built by the town doctor in a historic river town at the junction of Lake of the Ozarks and Truman Lake. The inn features homemade jams, breads, savory afternoon hors d'oeuvres and gourmet breakfasts prepared by Chef Henry. Warsaw has many attractions: 16 antique shops, historic swinging bridge, golf course, Missouri state fish hatchery, Truman Dam and visitor center. The inn also has beautiful flowerbeds, excellent bird and butterfly watching and a relaxing outdoor hot tub located on a private patio.

Rates at Victorian Garden Inn range from $65-$110.
Rates include a full breakfast.

Cranberry Crepes

This is our signature Christmas season recipe and looks festive on your favorite holiday plates! Crepes make the perfect accompaniment for soufflés when serving a fancy French country breakfast. For variation, the crepe can be served with strawberry or peach sauce. Crepes can be stuffed with filling and frozen for future use.

serves 12-14

Crepes:
1 cup cake flour, sifted
1/2 cup sugar
1/4 teaspoon salt
2 extra large eggs
1 ounce oil or clarified butter
1 orange rind, grated
8 ounces milk

Filling:
15 ounces ricotta cheese
1 orange rind, grated
juice from 1 orange
1/2 teaspoon salt
1 teaspoon vanilla
1 teaspoon triple sec or cointreau
1/4 cup powdered sugar
1/2 cup flour

Sauce:
1 cup orange juice
3/4 cup sugar
2 cups cranberries
1/4 cup water
2 Tablespoons corn starch
1/4 cup triple sec or cointreau

2 medium mixing bowls
1 8-inch nonstick skillet or crepe pan
1 9x13 inch baking dish
1 medium saucepan
Baking Time: 20 minutes
Baking Temperature: 350 °

Crepes:
Sift flour, sugar and salt together. Beat milk and eggs together. Combine wet and dry ingredients and mix until smooth. Add orange rind and oil to mixture and mix thoroughly. Let rest for 10-15 minutes.

Spray skillet with nonstick cooking spray. Heat skillet over medium high heat. Add 2 ounces batter and spread evenly around skillet. Cook 1-2 minutes and turn. Cook 1 minute and remove. Cool to room temperature. Place approximately 1/3 cup filling on crepe and roll up. Place in baking dish. Bake crepes at 350 ° for 20 minutes.

Filling:
Mix all ingredients well.

Sauce:
Bring orange juice and sugar to a boil. Add cranberries and cook until berries burst. Mix water and corn starch. Add to mixture and cook until thickened. Add triple sec. Top baked crepes with hot sauce mixture. Garnish with orange twists.

131

Victoria Gardens
Bed & Breakfast

1461 State Route BB
West Plains, MO 65775
(877)256-3268
www.victoria-gardens.com
laura@victoria-gardens.com

Hosts: John and Laura Dalton

Victoria Gardens Bed & Breakfast is a beautifully restored 1893 Victorian on 26 acres within city limits. It is elegantly decorated with the European antiques that we collected during our seven years in Great Britain. Guests may relax in our elegant living room or the less formal "teapot" room with large fireplace and television. During the spring, summer and fall, our wrap-around porch is a pleasant place to read, relax or nap in one of our sky chairs.

Our four spacious guest rooms include cable television, coffee and tea making facilities, private baths and European bed linens. Selected guest rooms feature whirlpool tubs, steam cabinet/shower combinations, sitting rooms and fireplaces.

We invite you to enjoy our four-course breakfast complete with home-made muffins, our signature "Hot Toddy Porridge" and followed by your choice of waffles, French toast, pancakes, omelets and other specialties.

Rates at Victoria Gardens range from $90-$135.
Rates include a full breakfast.

Hot Toddy Porridge

We serve 8 or 9 different porridges in the mornings, but Hot Toddy Porridge is a real favorite with our guests. Porridge served this way in Scotland would be called "Atholl Brose," which we encountered as both a breakfast dish and in a different form, a dessert. Serve a large bowl of porridge swirled with butter, sprinkled with natural coarse grain brown sugar and drizzled with a generous spoonful of whiskey. Not to be forgotten!

serves 4

4 servings prepared oatmeal
4 teaspoons bourbon
4 Tablespoons natural brown sugar, Turbinado sugar or Demarara sugar
4 teaspoons butter

Prepare 4 servings of your favorite oatmeal. Bob's Red Mill Scottish Oats is the most traditional (www.bobsredmill.com), but steel cut oats or Quaker rolled oats work equally well. No instant oatmeal, please!

Divide oatmeal evenly between four large cereal bowls or rimmed soup bowls.

Top each serving with butter and bourbon. Sprinkle with sugar and serve immediately.

Benner House
Bed & Breakfast

645 Main Street
Weston, MO 64098
(816)640-2616
http://ci.weston.mo.us
bennerbb@msn.com

Hosts: John and Julie Pasley

The Victorian Benner House in historic Weston is a fine example of steamboat gothic architecture built in 1898 by Mr. George Shawhan, who owned what we know today as the McCormick Distillery. The Benner House is ideally located just a pleasant walk from the downtown historic district which includes museums, antique shops, galleries, a winery, fine restaurants and an array of specialty shops for you to experience during your stay with us.

Your host and hostess, John and Julie Pasley, will make your visit to the Benner House a very special one. Return to a time when life moved at a slower pace. You may relax on the charming wrap-around porch, curl up in a rocking chair with your favorite book, warm up in front of the fire, luxuriate in the hot tub or take a refreshing dip in the swimming pool. All four rooms have private baths, one with a huge claw foot tub for your relaxation. You will enjoy a full candlelight breakfast in the Victorian dining room. Our signature dish is our cinnamon sticks, but we cannot share the recipe; you will have to come visit us to have these delectable pastries.

The Benner House is a perfect setting for your wedding, honeymoon, anniversary or just a very special time away.

Rates at the Benner House range from $90-$120.
Rates include a full breakfast.

Lil' Dixie Casserole

These are basically cheese grits, but no one ever knows they are grits. People have asked us what is in this casserole, and when we tell them grits, they are very surprised. One guest told us that his wife never eats grits, and she had just finished the entire casserole. This casserole can be made in a large 9x12 inch baking dish, but we find it looks better to serve to our guests in a large (8 ounce) ramekin. These grits are especially good on a cold morning.

serves 8

4 cups water
1 teaspoon salt
1 cup quick cooking grits
12 eggs, beaten
1 pound pork sausage, browned and well drained
1 1/2 cups sharp Cheddar cheese, shredded
1/2 cup milk
1/4 cup butter, cut into small pieces

1 medium mixing bowl (for eggs)
1 large saucepan
8 large (8 ounce) ramekins
1 large cookie sheet
Baking Time: 50 minutes
Baking Temperature: 350 °

In saucepan, bring water and salt to a boil. Stir in grits, reduce heat and cook 5 minutes, stirring constantly. Remove grits from heat and add a small amount of hot grits to the eggs. Return grits to heat, then add eggs. Stir in cooked sausage, 1 cup cheese, milk and butter. Stir until butter and cheese are melted.

Pour into 8 ramekins which have been sprayed with nonstick cooking spray. Sprinkle with remaining cheese and serve.

Hatchery House
Bed & Breakfast

618 Short Street
Weston, MO 64098
(816)640-5700
www.hatcherybb.com
hatcherybb@earthlink.net

Hosts: Bill and Anne Lane

Our Federal style home built in 1845 offers our guests a chance to step back in time and experience a more simple way of life. Each room has antiques, a gas log fireplace, a queen size bed and private bathroom. Some rooms have Jacuzzis, balconies or private entrances.

We are conveniently located within walking distance of shopping, a winery, fine dining and an Irish pub with live entertainment.

Rates at the Hatchery House range from $100-$150.
Rates include a full breakfast.

Cinnamon Encrusted Cream Cheese Coffee Cake

This delightful, lightly sweetened coffee cake helps you start your day off smiling and dreaming of something very special. This is a special recipe from Anne's friend, Melissa Solito. Many of our guests have asked for this recipe, so here it is.

makes 15 squares

2 packages of crescent rolls
2 packages (8 ounces each) cream cheese
1 3/4 cup sugar, divided
1 teaspoon vanilla
8 Tablespoons butter
1 Tablespoon cinnamon

1 medium mixing bowl
1 9x13 inch pan
1 round, flat plate
Baking Time: 30 minutes
Baking Temperature: 375 °

Spread one package of crescent roll triangles on bottom only of 9x13 inch pan. Pinch seams together. Set aside.

In medium mixing bowl, place cream cheese, 1 cup sugar and vanilla. Mix together on medium speed until smooth. Spread on top of crescent rolls. Top with remaining crescent roll triangles, pinching seams together. Set aside.

Mix remaining 3/4 cup sugar and cinnamon together. Sprinkle on top of crescent roll crust. Melt butter and pour over cinnamon and sugar topping.

Bake in a preheated 375 ° oven for 30 minutes. Cool for 2 hours or overnight in refrigerator.

Associate
Bed and Breakfast Inns

These inns are members of our association, but they have not been inspected yet. Because of this, we cannot guarantee that they meet the high standards of our association.

Beaver Creek
Bed & Breakfast

122 Campbell Ranch Road
Ava, MO 65608
(417)796-2102
beavercreekbandb@inter-linc.net

Hosts: Holly and Jerry Kadlubowski

Escape to your 1911 Country Victorian in the heart of the Ozarks with its out-of-the-way flavor. Located in Brownbranch, Beaver Creek Bed & Breakfast is a haven for canoeists, hikers and people who want quiet relaxation in a timeless world of yesterday. Enjoy Beaver and Caney Creeks meeting outside your door in one of three beautifully decorated rooms, each boasting its own theme. All rooms have private bathrooms (one with a Jacuzzi tub) and private entrances onto the front porch.

After a hearty country breakfast, enjoy a scenic canoe trip down Beaver Creek; hike or mountain bike on nearby Glade Top Trail in Mark Twain National Forest; stroll along lazy creek banks; browse our colorful flower gardens…or relax in the parlor with its river rock fireplace or the sitting room with its large bay window and unique river rock floor. This is your escape from modern day hustle and bustle…escape and relax.

Rates at Beaver Creek range from $60-$100.
Rates include a full country breakfast.

Mexican Nacho Soup

This soup is super easy to make! Since it starts with a box of au gratin potatoes, you don't have to peel or slice them. My husband requests this warm, filling and mildly spicy soup often.

serves 6-8

1 package (5 1/4 ounces) au gratin or julienne potatoes
1 can (15 1/4 ounces) fiesta corn, drained
1 can (14 1/2 ounces) diced tomatoes and green chilies
1 teaspoon Mexican seasoning
2 cups water
2 cups milk
1 pound Velveeta Mexican mild cheese, cubed
dash hot pepper sauce (optional)
minced fresh parsley (optional)

3 quart saucepan
Simmer Time: 15-20 minutes

In a 3 quart saucepan, combine the contents of the potato package, corn, tomatoes and water. Mix well, bringing to a boil.

Reduce heat. Cover and simmer for 15-18 minutes or until potatoes are tender. Add milk, cheese and Mexican seasoning.

Heat and stir often until the cheese is melted.

Garnish with hot sauce and parsley, if desired.

The Duck
A Lakeside Restaurant &
Bed & Breakfast Inn

599 Cherokee Road
Lake Ozark, MO 65049
(573)365-9973
www.theduckrestaurant.com
info@theduckrestaurant.com

Hosts: Mark Hooker and Donna Ziegler

The sun sets and a dim brilliance of color fills the evening sky and sparkles with a pink glow across the water. This will be your experience while dining or staying with us at our restaurant and soon to open Bed & Breakfast Inn.

Come take in our 180 ° view and enjoy a casual, relaxing fine dining experience. We feature steaks, chops, prime rib, seafood and pasta dishes. Our chef is continually working on new and tasty additions to our menu.

The Bed & Breakfast will open in fall 2002 with a large lakefront suite. Beautiful furnishings and linens will greet you upon entering, and a deck, Jacuzzi and fireplace will help you relax while viewing the spectacular sunsets. In the morning, awake to a scrumptious breakfast delivered to your door.

Romance abounds at our restaurant and inn. So bring that special someone and enjoy our "Sky Blue Pink" sunsets. We are located on beautiful Horseshoe Bend at the edge of Village of the Four Seasons. We are close to great golf courses, the factory outlet mall, several nice antique stores and fine shops.

Call us to book daytime meetings, private luncheons, showers or evening private parties.

Rates at The Duck are $150.
Rates include a full breakfast.

Steak Au Pouivre

Often served as a featured special, our guests have raved about this Kansas City strip steak studded with cracked black peppercorns, sautéed and finished with a brandy peppercorn sauce.

makes one steak

---

1 12-ounce Kansas City strip steak
cracked black pepper
8 ounces veal stock or demi-glaze (available at gourmet shops)
4 ounces heavy cream
2 ounces brandy
1 Tablespoon green peppercorns in brine, drained

1 medium sauté pan
Cooking Temperature: medium-high on stove top

Place medium sauté pan on medium heat.

While pan is heating, rub the Kansas City strip steak on both sides with cracked black pepper.

Place coated strip in hot pan and cook halfway to desired temperature.

Deglaze your pan with brandy, add veal stock or demi-glaze and reduce heat to medium.

Add heavy cream and drained green peppercorns.

Simmer steak until it is cooked to desired degree.

Remove steak to serving plate and spoon sauce over the top.

Another great recipe from The Duck:

Pesto & Prosciutto Pizza

This is a quick appetizer that pleases most palates, and guests are often surprised to find the base is a flour tortilla!

serves 2-3

1 10-inch flour tortilla (plain or flavored)
1-2 Tablespoons prepared or homemade pesto
1/8 cup chopped prosciutto
1/8 cup roma tomato, seeded and chopped
1/8 cup grated Parmesan-Reggiano cheese
1 Tablespoon toasted pine nuts

1 10-inch pizza pan or 1 pizza stone
Baking Time: 6-8 minutes
Baking Temperature: 425 °

Preheat oven to 425 °. If you have a pizza stone, let it preheat for at least 20 minutes—you want it good and hot.

Spread pesto on flour tortilla; use 1-2 Tablespoons pesto, depending on your taste.

Sprinkle with prosciutto and chopped tomato.

Cover all with grated Parmesan; use more than listed above if you like a lot of cheese.

Sprinkle with toasted pine nuts.

Transfer directly to pizza stone or put on pizza pan and bake for 6-8 minutes.

Cut into wedges and enjoy.

Another great recipe from The Duck:

Panna Cotta
(Italian Cooked Cream)

A cooking class in Florence, Italy, introduced us to the wonderful simplicity of Italian cooking. This dessert is easy and delicious. Once again, you'll be surprised at the results—cool and refreshing.

serves 6

4 cups whipping cream
1/2 cup sugar
2 teaspoons vanilla
2 envelopes Knox gelatin

Garnishes:
Choose from:
fresh berries
grapes
fruit coulis
warm chocolate sauce
crisp cookies

1 small mixing bowl
1 medium saucepan
6 6-ounce ramekins, custard cups or goblets

In a small mixing bowl, soften gelatin as directed on package.

Heat cream over low heat and add sugar; stir until dissolved. Add vanilla.

Stir in gelatin until melted.

Pour into serving bowls or goblets. Let cool.

Serve with fresh berries, fruit coulis or warm chocolate sauce.

For a lighter recipe, use 1/2 milk and 1/2 cream.

Never let cream and gelatin come to a boil. It won't set up.

A Planter's Wheel
Bed & Breakfast Inn

1112 4th Street
PO Box 78
Platte City, MO 64079
(816)858-2079 or 866-437-2079
www.aplanterswheel.com
karon@aplanterswheel.com

Hosts: Wilbur and Karon Roberts

This dramatic style residence in Platte City was quality built by Judge A.D. Burns, Circuit Judge for Platte County in the 1890s. This small town, just minutes from the Kansas City International Airport, is conveniently located near many historical sites and recreational destinations. Within 25 minutes, you can find yourself at the new NASCAR track in Kansas City, Kansas, Worlds of Fun Entertainment Park, Country Club Plaza shopping district, or historic St. Joseph, Missouri. Historic Weston, Missouri, and Fort Leavenworth, Kansas, are only a short ten minutes away.

The house has high ceilings, large stately rooms, a walk-in attic and a large concrete basement. Built from stone, the foundation is more than two feet wide. All of the woodwork is made from Red Gum, which looks like walnut. Each board cut for the house is branded with Judge A.D. Burns on the backside. Large open rooms make it a great house for meetings, weddings and family reunions or a quiet place for business people to relax after an enjoyable day in Kansas City. The house is equipped with internet access for business clientele. The Judge's dining room will hold table seating for more than 30 people.

This house is more than 100 years old but, remarkably, has had only four owners before the Roberts's. Platte County owned the house for more than 40 years, using the structure as office space. Some of the county services housed here included the rationing board, the University of Missouri Extension offices, police station and county adoption office.

Rates at A Planter's Wheel range from $80-$135.
Rates include a full breakfast.

Tara's Favorite Breakfast Pizza

I had my own child care center for several years. A student by the name of Tara brought me this recipe, and it was a hit for preschoolers and staff. We kept this as a family favorite.

serves 6-8

2 packages refrigerator crescent rolls
1 pound favorite sausage, browned and drained
1/2 of large bag of shredded hash browns, frozen
6 eggs, slightly beaten
1 cup shredded cheese (Colby, Cheddar or Mozzarella)
1/2 cup grated Parmesan cheese

1 2-quart bowl
1 measuring cup
shredder (optional)
1 8-inch skillet
1 pizza pan or stone
luncheon plates
Baking Time: 25-30 minutes
Baking Temperature: 350 °

Spread crescent rolls individually to cover the bottom of a large pizza pan or stone. Brown and drain sausage. Layer sausage over rolls.

Layer remaining ingredients in the following order:
hash browns
eggs
shredded cheese
Parmesan cheese

Place in 350 ° oven and bake until crust is brown and eggs are cooked, approximately 25-30 minutes. Let set at room temperature for 3 to 5 minutes. Cut and serve.

KD's Botanical Guest House Bed & Breakfast

2005 Vichy Road
Rolla, MO 65401
(573)308-1013
kdhall@fidnet.com

Host: Ms. Gerry Hall

KD's Botanical Guest House is a retreat from the busy world in a park-like setting with perennial flower gardens. It is the perfect place for a peaceful walk or spending time on a bench watching birds. You can find all of this in the city of Rolla, just off of the UMR campus. The Civil War era farmhouse has the charm of the older home with a hot tub on the back porch for the perfect ending of the day.

To accommodate the comfort of guests, KD's B&B is planned for the peace and quiet of adults. Guest rooms are upstairs. Smoking is permitted outside only. No pets are allowed. There is a resident cat on the property.

Rates at KD's Botanical Guest House range from $60-$100.
Rates include a light & healthy breakfast with in season fruits, breads and coffee/tea.

Custard Rhubarb Pie

My mother always had a rhubarb pie in the house. A long row of rhubarb grew along her garden.

serves 6-8

1 9 inch unbaked pie shell
1 1/2 cups cubed rhubarb
1 cup sugar
2 Tablespoons flour
2 eggs
2 Tablespoons butter, melted
2 Tablespoons milk
1 teaspoon vanilla
tiny pinch salt

1 medium mixing bowl
1 large mixing bowl
1 9 inch pie pan
6-8 dessert plates
Baking Time: 45-60 minutes
Baking Temperature: 350 °

Place sifter in medium bowl; add dry ingredients. Set aside.

In a large bowl, beat eggs with a whisk; add butter, milk and vanilla. Add dry ingredients to mixture and stir well. Stir in rhubarb.

Pour mixture into pie shell. Bake in a 350 ° preheated oven for 45-60 minutes.

Directory of Missouri Bed & Breakfast
Association Membership
Bold type: Inns listed in this book

City	Inn/Phone/Website
City	*Inn/Phone/Website*
Bonne Terre	**Victorian Veranda, 573/358-1134, 800/343-1134**
Bonnots Mill	**Dauphine Hotel B&B Inn, 573/897-4144, 877/901-4144, www.dauphinehotel.com**
Boonville	Morgan Street Repose, 660/882-7195, 800/248-5061, www.bbim.org/morganrepose
Bourbon	Wildflower Inn, 573/468-7975, www.ne3.com/flowers/
Branson	**Aunt Sadie's Garden Glade B&B, 417/335-4063, 800/944-4250, www.auntsadies.com**
Branson	Barger House, 417/335-2134, 800/266-2134, www.bargerhouse.com
Branson	Branson Hotel B&B, 417/335-6104, 800/933-0651, www.bransonhotelbb.com
Branson	Branson House B&B, 417/334-0959, www.bransonhouseinn.com
Branson	Brass Swan B&B, 417/336-3669, 800/280-6873, www.brassswan.com
Branson	Josie's Peaceful Getaway, 417/338-2978, 800/289-4125, www.bbim.org/josies
Branson	Lakeshore B & B, 417/338-2698, 800/285-9739, www.lakeshorebandb.com
Branson West	Martindale B & B, 417/338-2588, 888/338-2588, www.bbim.org/martindale
Branson/Hollister	**Red Bud Cove, 417/334-7144, 800/677-5525, www.redbudcove.com**
Branson/Ridgedale	**Canna Cove Bed and Breakfast, 417/779-3385, 877/877-3886, www.bbonline.com/mo/cannacove/**
Camdenton	**Castleview, 573/346-9818, 877/346-9818, www.lakelinks.com/castleview**
Cape Girardeau	**Bellevue Bed & Breakfast, 573/335-3302, 800/768-6822, www.bbim.org/bellevue**
Cape Girardeau	Rose Bed Inn, 573/332-7673, 866/767-3233, www.rosebedinn.com
Carthage	Grand Avenue, 417/358-7265, 888/380-6786, www.grand-avenue.com
Columbia	Gathering Place, 573/815-0606, 877/731-6888, www.gatheringplacebb.com
Columbia	**Missouri Manor, 573/499-4437, www.missourimanor.com**
Columbia	**University Avenue B & B, 573/499-1920, 800/499-1920, www.bbim.org/universityave**
Commerce	Anderson House, 573/264-4123, 800/705-1317, www.rosecity.net/andersonhouse
Dixon	**Rock Eddy Bluff Farm, 573/759-6081, 800/335-5921, www.rockeddy.com**
Ethel	**Recess Inn, 660/486-3328, 800/628-5003**
Excelsior Springs	Inn on Crescent Lake, 816/630-6745, www.crescentlake.com
Fordland	**Red Oak Inn, 816/767-2444, www.theredoakinn.com**
Fulton	**Loganberry Inn, 573/642-9229, 888/866-6661, www.loganberryinn.com**
Fulton	Romancing the Past, 573/592-1996, www.romancingthepast.com
Hannibal	**Garth Woodside Mansion, 573/221-2789, 888/427-8409, www.garthmansion.com**
Hannibal	**Lulabelle's, 573/221-6662, 800/882-4890, www.lulabelles.com**
Hannibal	**Reagan's Queen Anne, 573/221-0774, 888/221-1251, www.bbhost.com/reagansqueenanne**
Hermann	**Nestle Inn, 573/486-5893, 800/700-9980, www.nestleinn.com**
Hollister	**Cameron's Crag, 417/335-8134, 800/933-8529, www.camerons-crag.com**
Independence	Woodstock Inn B & B, 816/833-2233, 800/276-5202, www.independence-missouri.com
Ironton	**Parlor Bed and Breakfast, 573/546-2670, www.theparlorbandb.com**
Jackson	**Trisha's Bed and Breakfast, 573/243-7427, 800/651-0408, www.rosecity.net/trishabb**
Jamesport	Country Colonial, 660/684-6711, www.jamesport-mo.com/countrycolonialnl
Jefferson City	Cliff Manor Bed and Breakfast Inn, 573/635-4208, 877/538-9616, www.cliffmanor.com
Jefferson City	**Huber's Ferry B & B, 573/455-2979, 877/454-2979, www.bbonline.com/mo/hubersferry/**
Jefferson City	Jefferson Inn B & B, 573/635-7196, 800/530-5009, www.bbim.org/jefferson
Joplin	**Prosperity School B&B, 417/673-0833, www.joplinbedandbreakfast.com**
Kansas City	**Dome Ridge B & B, 816/532-4074**
Kansas City	LaFontaine Inn B & B, 816/753-4434, 888/832-6000, www.lafontainebb.com
Kansas City	**Su Casa B & B, 816/965-5647, www.sucasabb.com**
Kearney	**Western Way B&B, 816/628-5686**
Kimmswick	**Wenom Drake House, 636/464-1983, www.bbim.org/wenomdrake**
Kirksville	Brashear House B & B, 660/627-0378, www.communities.msn.com/BrashearHouseBedBreakfast/